SUPER NES IS HERE!

So you thought you'd seen it all—the unforget-
table antics of Mario, the awesome action of
Castlevania, the incredible gameplaying of doz-
ens of great EIGHT-BIT Nintendo games out
there across the nation, on your block, in your
TV set!

Now, along come SIXTEEN-BIT Nintendo
games—games with truly stunning visual
graphics, games of previously unimaginable
complexity, entertainment, and challenge! If
there's nothing like the excitement of a great
Nintendo game, you better believe you've never
done it all 'til you've encountered the games of
SUPER NES!

Jeff Rovin has spent uncounted hours behind
closed doors playing the games of Super NES—
examining them, analysing them, and learning
their secrets—so that he can now come to you
with tactics, tips, and strategies on how to be
your best at sixteen bits—and how to have more
fun with the Super Nintendo Entertainment System than you could ever have guessed!

D0556164

St. Martin's Paperbacks titles
by Jeff Rovin

HOW TO WIN AT NINTENDO GAMES

HOW TO WIN AT NINTENDO GAMES 2

HOW TO WIN AT NINTENDO GAMES 3

HOW TO WIN AT NINTENDO GAMES 4

HOW TO WIN AT NINTENDO SPORTS GAMES

HOW TO WIN AT SUPER MARIO BROS. GAMES

HOW TO WIN AT SEGA & GENESIS GAMES

HOW TO WIN AT GAME BOY GAMES

HOW TO WIN AT SUPER NINTENDO ENTERTAINMENT
SYSTEM GAMES

THE UNAUTHORIZED TEENAGE MUTANT
NINJA TURTLES QUIZ BOOK

SIMPSON FEVER!

St. Martin's Paperbacks titles are available at quantity dis-
counts for sales promotions, premiums or fund raising. Special
books or book excerpts can also be created to fit specific
needs.

For information write to special sales manager, St. Martin's
Press, 175 Fifth Avenue, New York, N.Y. 10010.

HOW TO
WIN
AT
SUPER
NINTENDO®
ENTERTAINMENT SYSTEM
GAMES
Jeff Rovin

ST. MARTIN'S PAPERBACKS

NOTE: If you purchased this book without a cover you should be aware that this book is stolen property. It was reported as 'unsold and destroyed' to the publisher, and neither the author nor the publisher has received any payment for this 'stripped book'.

How to Win at Super Nintendo® Entertainment System Games is an unofficial guide, not endorsed by Nintendo®.

Nintendo is a registered trademark, and Super NES is a trademark, of Nintendo of America, Inc.

HOW TO WIN AT SUPER NINTENDO ENTERTAINMENT SYSTEM GAMES

Copyright © 1992 by Jeff Rovin.

All rights reserved. No part of this book may be used or reproduced in any manner whatsoever without written permission except in the case of brief quotations embodied in critical articles or reviews. For information address St. Martin's Press, 175 Fifth Avenue, New York, N.Y. 10010.

ISBN: 0-312-92871-8

Printed in the United States of America

St. Martin's Paperbacks edition/May 1992

10 9 8 7 6 5 4 3 2

CONTENTS

ACTRAISER

Type: Fantasy quest.

Objective: Tanzra, the evil one, has chased the benevolent Master off the world to his Sky Palace, enabling wickedness to girdle the globe. Centuries pass and though virtually powerless, the Master resolves to return to the fallen realm and confront Tanzra and his minions. But victory won't be easy: there are six lands to conquer, and each of them is heavily guarded. Each land is divided into two Action modes with a Simulation mode. The Action modes enable you to recapture lands; in the Simulation mode you nurture the land and build the Master's strength.

Hero: The Master begins the game without much: during the Action modes the lord inhabits a mighty warrior statue which has a sword and the ability to jump, kneel, or attack. An Angel helps you through the Simulation stages of gameplay. During the Simulation mode, you can also move your Sky Palace to any location on the map.

Along the way, in both modes, you acquire magic spells, power-ups, and various additional weapons that can be used in that mode (Act bonuses during

Acts, Simulation acquisitions during Simulations). The Simulation powers include Acts of Nature, which range from mild Lightning to destructive Earthquakes. The more powerful Acts can only be used as your power increases. Your former subjects will also help you with offerings of various kinds.

Enemies: Flying, walking, crawling, and slithering monsters of all kinds, including bosses at the end of each land.

Menu: There's only the one game, which can be saved. The player can also erase it at any point.

Scoring: Progress in the game is rewarded with an increase in your power and in the number of subjects who have returned to the fold. You're playing against a timer during the Act scenes, so don't tarry!

Strategies: Here's the land-by-land strategy.

Fillmore, Act 1: Select this land first. Jump into the Tree; when you reach the Tree with a face, leap and hit it once, then go to the right to avoid its fireballs, and kill it with two more blows. A great many bonuses will show up to help you along. Hit the power-up items as you travel; the first will contain 500 points, the second a 1-Up, the third a Whole Apple, the fourth a 1-Up, the fifth another Whole Apple (one, two, and five are all up in the trees). Use the Ozlike Trees here to hitch a ride across the thorns. When you face Centaurus, lure him to the left, crouch just to the left of the tree that's in the background—kneel right in the middle of the dirt area—and hit it, though not so close that it can knee you. When its scepter lights up, run left and hug the ledge to get out of range of its bolts. Repeat until the horseman is dead.

Simulation: Save your game, then use Lightning to burn away the Bushes above the house—not the Forest to the bottom right; Lightning won't work there. Build the road to the upper left bat symbol. Fight the Napper Bats using the Angel's arrows (Y button) while the town is built around the road; lead your people as they complete each section. Position your Angel over the Symbol, slightly to the left—at the M in Fillmore—and blast each Napper Bat that emerges from the Symbol *or* Blue Dragon that flies up from the bottom. Direct the people over the Symbol so they can seal it, and allow the building to continue. Take their Bomb offering. After the Symbol is sealed, head to the Symbol in the east and do the same. You'll be directed, then, to blast a specific rock below the cliffs; do so and use the Magic Fire you get to fight monsters.

Use Lightning to clear the Bushes south of the Palace, then continue building. Seal the Symbol to the south, and your people will acquire the skill of Bridge building. Use this to go west from the Palace—after clearing the Bushes with Lightning—cross the River, and seal the Blue Dragons' lair, using your Angel to blast any of the winged reptiles that emerge.

You'll be told to face Minotaurus next, which means that after you finish building towns throughout undeveloped Fillmore, you must return to the Sky Palace, use the *Fight Monsters* order, and begin—

Fillmore, Act II: General notes: deal with monsters you encounter before continuing, since you don't want to scroll new ones onto the screen before you've gotten rid of the old ones. Also, if you're fighting projectile-firing monsters—especially the Skulls—drop down to lower ledges when they're about to fire *or* leap up to draw their fire in that direction, then slash from below them (where possible) or charge.

To begin, jump all the way down the shaft. Kill the

two Harpies you encounter, then leap the Spikes and crouch on the opposite ledge. After the Gnome has fired, kill it. When you face the fireball-spitting Skull, you can start climbing or go straight ahead. The climb will give you bonuses as described below; going ahead gets you through the Act quicker. If you climb, the first two bonuses are 1000 points each. Continuing up and right, when you reach the top ledge go left to the ledge below it and drop down the shaft to get a Whole Apple in the next bonus. Continue to the left and descend back to where you found the first bonus. Go right (which is where you'd have gone if you'd avoided the climb), drop down the shaft, and go left to get another Whole Apple—you *can* jump over the pit of Spikes if you stand on the very edge of the ledge and leap.

Continue right, watching out for the Spikes that rise from the floor and for the Harpies who want to knock you onto the left Spike. Climb: the bonus on the left contains a 1-Up, on the right 1000 points. Climb and get ready to exit right—if you have time, there's a Half Apple up a bit, to the right. Before you can exit, however, there's a skeletal monster you'll have to defeat: be ready to leap over it whenever it charges. Six hits will kill it. After you beat it, a door will open on the right; enter, climb—watching out for the Lava Balls, which, fortunately, you can destroy—and get the Whole Apple in the bonus on top. When you've got that, race through to avoid the falling Spikes and make ready to face Minotaurus.

The giant will leap up and off the screen: move around, avoiding the giant when he lands, and leap the Axe the creature will throw. Move in and get in your blows. Minotaurus will leap again; repeat. When you move in, Minotaurus has no defenses and is relatively easy to slay.

Bloodpool, Act 1: Start the battle by heading right. The first bonus is 1000 points. The Logs only float for a second, so get off them fast. Also, kill the metal birds that come at you; otherwise they'll resurface when you get on the Logs and knock you off. The second bonus is a Half Apple; the third is a 1-Up, but you'd better cross the Bridge to its right quickly, because it collapses. The fourth bonus is a Whole Apple; the Bridge to its right also collapses. When you face the boss, the Manticore, go to the ledge on the top right, then drop to the ledge below it. Jump the blasts the monster fires from the left—it fires once at each of the three ledges; you only have to jump the ones it shoots at your ledge. Manticore will return to the top right ledge then; when it does, you'll be under it, able to hack away. Repeat as often as necessary.

Simulation: This time there are Napper Bats and Red Demons, so hold them off as you build to the west. When the monsters' lair is sealed, use Sun to dry up the Marshes below the Palace, and build below the River to seal the Symbol of the Blue Dragons—keep them at bay from the left side, firing right at them: you'll have more room to maneuver in case one escapes. You'll have to use the Bridge offering here, as these rubes have obviously forgotten how to build 'em since they erected the last town. One Bridge use will ford the River.

Before you can do much more building, you'll have to go find Teddy. He's in the cave to the east of the Lake; give him the Bread, and you'll get a magic Skull in return. It will be needed to seal a Symbol that can't be sealed any other way. Continue building to the south—Bridges can now be built without your help— and seal the Blue Dragon lair below. You'll get a Bomb from the lair. You'll also get a hidden 1-Up by causing it to rain in the woods northeast of the Blood-pool Lake.

Next, head below the Lake and blast the Bushes there, to reveal the last Red Demons' lair. Use the Skull to close it up, and the Lake will be cleansed. Unfortunately, Teddy's gotten into trouble again and you'll have to go to the Castle to save him.

Bloodpool, Act II: Go ahead to the Elevator and take it down; the bonus on the left, as you descend, is the Origin of Magic. Ride back up once you've got it— don't ride *down* into the Electrical barrier, below—and head right. Descend at the shaft and go right—watching out for all the floating Skulls that will attack. Go ahead in the room where the lights come and go; you can drop down one ledge safely when you start here. The bonus on the right, below, is a Whole Apple. Climb when you exit, watching out for the three Gels, and go right. Cross the suspended ledges quickly, since they fall after a moment; miss one and you die. Fight the four flame-breathing Gargoyles by crouching on the steps below the platform of each of the little killers and slashing up. When you reach the bottom, the monster on the ground is tough to kill because of its long tongue: don't give it a chance to extend it! Run toward it and hit it. If you fail, still hack at the creature, taking a hit or two before it dies. Go right and you'll reach two Electrical barriers: leap when they're down. You'll come to another Elevator; use it to hop onto the column in the middle or over to the right-side Elevator, and ride it up. (Just don't ride the first Elevator *down*. That's another Electrical barrier below you.) There's a 1-Up in the bonus on the top left. Don't tarry about leaping left to get it: within moments, you'll hit the Spiked ceiling and die. After you get the prize, go down and up again and exit top right.

After crossing the top of the Castle—killing the blue creatures lest they clobber you when you stop to fight the Gargoyles—enter the room on the right. Hit the bony monster as before, with one swift hack, and climb: you can only stand on the Logs when they're lit. The bonus here contains a Whole Apple. Go right on top and face the Zeppelin Wolf. Jump between the lowest and middle of the three fireballs when they're thrown, and then get as far from the wizard as you can . . . unless he's on one of the two middle-sized columns. In that case, get under and behind him and hack away after the fireballs are gone. When he dematerializes, return to the middle and watch to see where he shows up. If he's on the ground, lowest, or topmost column, stay away from him completely. If he's on the middle column, jump the fireballs as before and go under and behind him. Hit him while he's shooting his first and second bolts; run before the third comes your way. He'll turn into a Werewolf when his power is half drained; don't attack unless you're under him, and make sure you hit the Werewolf heads that fly from the sides of the screen. (If you get in enough hits when he's still the Wizard, you can jump down and hack at the Werewolf while he's forming; when he's fully transformed, you'll take a few hits, but you can polish the creature off before he runs and starts firing Werewolf heads.)

When you emerge, you'll find that your subjects have been quarreling. That means a trip to the next locale and a search for Harmonious Music!

Kasandora, Act I: The creature on the first Skull throws spears to the left and right, so be careful. The Thorn Bushes under it are deadly, so leap them. When you reach the second Skeleton, a Tentacle Plant rises from beneath the Rib just left of the longest one. You can avoid it simply by getting onto the Skull and running along the Skeleton's back. After the rippling Dune, another Tentacle Plant rises from the sand, spitting projectiles, so take your finger off the controller, letting your hero just slide right, and start swinging as you slip down the right side of the Dune: two hacks will kill it. Another Tentacle follows the next Dune. Stay on top of the sand dishes ahead to avoid more Tentacles, but watch out for the creatures on top and the fireballs that fly by, dropping little fireballs on you. Hack at them to destroy them. There's a Whole Apple in the bonus on the ground after the three dishes. Two more Tentacles, a few ogres, and you can enter the building at the end. Just make sure your first big leap is a good one, or you die.

Once you're through the door, watch out for the flying monsters that drop suddenly while you're crossing the columns. When you get on the first two columns, wait on the left side till the creature has descended on the right, then kill it. There are just two. When you reach the tower, giant bugs fly from the windows, so don't jump ahead until they're back in their hives. Once they're in, jump, run to the middle of the tower's lower level, and hack left and right at the bugs when they emerge. Repeat for the second tower, then climb and get the Origin of Magic on top. Make your way down and jump to the column on the right—or, when you're more experienced, take a giant leap from the top of the second tower to the third. The next bonus, on the column to the right (invisible, below your screen) is a 1-Up. On top of the fourth tower there's a Whole Apple. However, you can only reach it by leaping right from the very top of the third tower. Drop down to the right, where there's a sand dish with an ogre on it and a fireball above it. (Or, if you wish, take a mighty rightward leap from the fourth tower: you'll pass the dish entirely.) After the ruins and the Tentacle ahead, there's a Whole Apple and the boss, Dagoba. Get right in front of the beast as it rises from the sands, where its projectiles will do no damage. Hack away. When it submerges, its pincers will rake down toward you; leap to the left when they're right beside you, and keep running in that direction to keep from sliding into them. When they submerge, turn and fight the monster from in front again. Repeat.

Simulation: Rain two sections right and one up to uncover the Napper Bat lair, then build your town over it. Stay above the lair, shooting down, to get both the Bats and the Demons who are coming from the south. Next, build east to cover the lair there, then to the north—where you'll uncover a lair using rain on the desert—then move northeast. You'll uncover a Pyramid before you reach the lair: cause an earthquake and a 1-Up will be given to you. Build on the Pyramid, then continue to the east. When you've sealed that Symbol, you'll learn another secret about the Pyramid. Before you go fight the monster therein, do some more building. (You can't finish, but you can get *some* work done.)

Kassandora, Act II: Crouch to kill the Asps, and hit the Pharoah Head three times to destroy it. The Mummies are easy to kill with one swipe, but when you face the Blue Guardian, step left, out of range, when he stops moving, because that means he's about to take a serious lunge in your direction! Enter the door and drop down the slides, watching out for the Pharaoh Heads. Go left, past the Scorpion—which fires projectiles from its tail—and climb. Halfway up, jump to the left for an Origin of Magic. Go right to the Elevator, take it to the top, then go left on the Elevators. The top left bonus is a 1-Up. Drop off the bottom Elevator and glide left to the ledge. Go left.

Kill the Scorpion, fight the Blue Light, and go up the Elevator; the bonus on the right is a Whole Apple. Leap to it when the Scorpion is facing right, kill it, and get the bonus. Go left on the Elevators and up to the door on the right, killing the Scorpions and Blue Light there. Enter the door, make your way past the Blue Guardians and Asps, and the balls that drop from the spouts overhead. (If you leap over the blue triggers in the floor, you'll be okay.) Climb the steps, hacking at the Pharaoh Heads as necessary, go left at the top, killing the Asps, kill the Heads—if you don't, you won't be able to wait for the Mummy on top to leave, and it'll knock you back down—and attack the Mummies as you move right on top. When you come to the slide, go down slowly and leap to the right at the bottom, to the Elevator. (You can run back up the slope, somewhat, to wait for the Elevator.) Kill the Blue Guardian on top, get a Whole Apple from the bonus ahead, and continue left. When you face the Red Guardian, wait until it fires its Swords. Leap them, and when the warrior jumps right, you hurry left. Now you're in the chamber of Pharoah.

You've got to avoid the giant mask when it comes crashing to the floor, and hack at it when it does, leaping the fireballs it fires and the Arrows that come from the walls. You can destroy the Arrows, but not the fireballs.

When you win here, you'll be rewarded with Harmonious Music, which you should use to calm things in Bloodpool—simply by accessing it there. You'll be rewarded with several goodies, including a Compass. Return to Kasandora when you're done and learn that your people are suffering from plague. To find it, you must journey to Marahna . . . but not yet.

Aitos, Act 1: Go right, leaping the traps when they fall, and ride the Birds up to the second Lava Pool. (You can stay on further, but you'll miss the Whole Apple.) To get back on the Birds, wait until the flying demon —flinging mini-Tornadoes—backs off to the right somewhat; just use your sword on the little winds and you'll be safe. Hack at the Flying Skulls and leap onto the cliff beyond. Leap the rolling Spores, get the 500 points, and go down the ledges. There's 1000 points on the bottom left; when you've got it, go right. Drop off the ledge—there's a Tornado demon, but it's no trouble—and go right. Cross the Waterfall: the first bonus is Crush, the second a Whole Apple, and the third Projectiles. (You can get the latter by attacking from the ledge to its lower right and jumping up at it.) Next up: the Dragon.

Go to the fourth ledge in, flinging Projectiles and using Magical Stardust, and you'll have no trouble.

Simulation: Giant Skull Heads are a new nemesis here, to the tune of eight Arrows each to kill; unless you use your Strength of Angel offering, in which case it'll take two arrows. Clear the land—rocks and bushes alike, using Lightning—and keep killing Skull Heads, or nothing will get built! You'll also want to close its lair first . . . the one to the west of the Palace. Note: you can't seal the lair in the northwest until you learn mountaineering skills, which will come with time and the sealing of the other Symbols.

When the area is settled, it's time to go into the Volcano to do battle.

Aitos, Act II: This time you're going left, then down to the right. Go slowly: you have to eliminate each enemy as it appears. If you let more than two collect, you'll have trouble right here in lava city! Enter the door and kill the Eyeball before you try to cross the ledges. (Note: you can only slay the Eyeball monster when its several eyes collect into one.) Keep jumping to the right, as the ledges lower into the Lava! When the ledges sink, you *can* leap up and stay aloft until they rise . . . but that's a risky maneuver. Better to jump ahead when they're on the rise, get onto the highest one to the right—it doesn't submerge—then finish the crossing when the other ledges are rising. Enter the door at the end.

The Bridge ahead has collapsing sections, so cross by landing only on sections over support columns. You can destroy the arrows the Knights up ahead are firing. The first bonus is Origin of Magic. Kill the creature from underneath the ledge to get rid of it. Go down the shaft beyond and drop past the first Firehead—it's on the right. You'll land atop another one—on the left. Get off quickly by going down and to the right, or you'll be fried. There's a Whole Apple in the bonus beyond. Get it and drop off *quickly* to the right. Go left at the bottom and face the Firewheel. Your Magical Stardust alone should be enough to destroy it.

Now that this region has been settled, it's time to take care of old business by going to—

Marahna, Act I: Landing on the island to the south, you must fight once again. Step on the rocks to cross the water, climb the structure, go right and top, drop down one level, go left, and get the Whole Apple. Drop down a level, go right, and get the Source of Magic. Head left—crouching to fight the Spear Carriers—and drop down into the mists. Go right and enter the door. When you emerge, cross the water, go up the structure to the top, continue across the top until you get the 1-Up—watching out for the Snakes that drop from overhead when you try to cross. When you get the extra life, go right and polish off all the monsters on this level. When they're gone, go left and get the Whole Apple. Go right, through the waters, to the next structure, and enter the door to fight the boss, the plant Rafflasher. (If you get the Whole Apple earlier, you'll lose hit points on your way to the doorway. Better to face the boss fully powered!)

You've got to stand directly underneath it—not even on the rock, but to the right of that—and attack its mouth by leaping at it . . . and calling on Magical Stardust. When the Tentacle attacks, leap it and run to the left to escape it, regroup, and attack anew when it's submerged. Rafflasher's Fireballs can be destroyed with your sword.

Simulation: Use Lightning and Sun to clear the Palm Trees and water, respectively. Keep killing monsters here or you won't be able to build much. When you get the Herb, return to Kasandora.

At Kasandora, use the Herbs, and you'll be given an Ancient Tablet. Finish settling the land, then return to Marahna.

At Marahna use the Ancient Tablet and the people will organize an expedition to the bird-shaped island in the northeast—watch the boat set sail! Go ahead and use Lightning on the trees just east of the "head" of the bird. Meanwhile, continue developing the land, closing the lair in the southwest. On the island, your bold crew will discover Magical Aura and they'll give it to you. Give them Compass in return, then head to—

Northwall, *Act I:* Armed with Magical Aura, descend and go right, watching out for the Icicle pits. An Origin of Magic is the first bonus. Run quickly across the Ice Bridge—it'll collapse—scale the cliff, and enter the door. No toughies thus far. In the room, watch out for the Eyeballs that shoot out in your direction, be that horizontal, vertical, or diagonal. At the end of the trail, leap the cliff and struggle up on the other side for a 1000 point bonus. Go down.

Go left on the Iceberg, standing on the far left, and hack at the Gargoyle when you reach the left. Get a Whole Apple from the bonus, then return to the right. Don't ride the Icebergs to the right *yet:* just leap the Icicle sticking out and get the 1-Up from the bonus on the bottom of the pond. Continue right, kill the monster if you want—he'll return in any case— then go left and get on the Iceberg. (You'll reach it from the second step . . . not the top step.) Duck while you're riding the second so the Icicles don't clip you. Kill the monster, then continue right into the door.

Catch the Ice-coaster, but jump off it at the end or you'll die. Jump to the ledge on the upper left to get a bonus of 1000 points, then continue up. Next bonus, above: Crush. Climb up to the right, drop down off the ledge on top (to the right), and climb the ice ledges on the right. Go left, climb—facing more monsters than you'll ever want to see—but be safe and use your Magical Aura here. Go left at the top and get a Whole Apple, then head right. Enter the room and face the boss: the Merman Fly. Use your Aura here to get in a few licks, but you shouldn't have much trouble in any case: get on the side of the monster that has the most room, and just edge toward that side while the Fly drops four series of bombs straight down. After that, the creature will descend and you can hack— provided you've positioned yourself on one of the raised areas of the ground. Repeat.

Simulation: There are pairs of Skull Heads here, so you'd best get your supercharged Bow out. Use Sun to melt the snow and build a path due east to close up the first Skull Symbol, which is covered by snow. Close up the first and you'll get a much-needed

Strength of Angel. Give the people here the Sheep's Fleece when they complain, then keep the last Skull pinned down (as each new one emerges from its northeast lair) so more land can be developed—specifically in the northwest. Close that Symbol, and your people will learn how to build Bridges, enabling you to close the second Skull hole. (Don't worry about the Ice around this Symbol: you can build right over it.) When all of the lairs are sealed, it's time for—

Northwall, Act II: Armed with Magical Aura, head left. Go up the cliff for a 1-Up, then slide back down into the pit. Drop down the opening and go left for a Half Apple and, below it, 500 points. Head right, enter the passageway and climb the Tree. Ascend on the left side, and when the Bird drops the Worm, hurry up and off of the Limb with the Worm. Face right and kill the Bird, go up to the middle Limb, and kill the ogre to the upper right before continuing. Repeat the Bird maneuver on the right, then kill the ogre overhead on the right—while standing on the Limb in the middle. Exit right, kill the Eyeball at the end, and go up. Go up again at the first opening, go left, kill the ogre, jump to the middle Limb, and then to the one above it on the left. Leap over the Mini-Bubbles into the hollow Limb beyond. Kill the ogre, continue left, get the 1000 points, and go right. Kill the ogre on the right—the hollow Limb beyond is empty—ascend, kill the ogre on the left, ascend, kill the ogre on the right, and continue up. When you come to a region with two ogres, one on either side, you're at the end. Kill the one on the right—you can get him from the Limb below—and ascend into a room with short-lived Purple Bubbles and longer-lived (but not by much) Green Bubbles. And if you thought climbing the disappearing Logs was a pain—

Ride the Green Bubble up on the left side, get over to one in the middle, and get off on the rightside Limb with the ogre on it—sorry, you have to, but at least you can hack at him as you rise. Hop to the left side and continue riding up on a Green Bubble, jumping onto the next Green Bubble you see coming up on your right the *instant* it appears—otherwise, your current Bubble will pop and you'll drop! Get off on the Vine on the left of the internal stalk of the Tree and climb, killing the ogre on the right, then ride up to the next ogre-Limb, and go left, hopscotching from a Purple Bubble to a Green Bubble on the left side. Ride up, get off on the next Vine, and climb out of there to the snowy surface of the Tree.

It's time to face the Arctic Wyvern. Stand on a high point and get behind it when it swoops low; it can only fire forward. Use Magical Aura when you can't get to it, and you'll inflict enough damage to beat it.

When you're finished here, go back to—

Marahna, where you'll cause an Earthquake so the mainland and island in the northwest will become connected, and the last Symbol can be closed. The people will tell you to go to the Shrine, where bad tidings awaits. Namely, that you can begin the long overdue—

Marahna, Act II: Virtually every avenue is equally deadly, so make your way through slowly.

Beat the last demon by using Aura to batter the creature; by getting behind it to avoid its fire—though not so you're under the falling Spikes on the left—and by hacking at it when it alights.

When the monster dies, its island will emerge from the sea. That's Death Heim, and it's your last stop. All you have to do to get through here is fight every boss you fought in the game, again, one after the other . . . only they move *faster* now than they did before.

And when you're done with them, you have to battle Tanzra. Armed with Projectiles and Aura, stand at the left, avoiding the creature's fire. When the giant head comes down, shoot your Projectiles to the right. Move right when it shifts, leaping up to get between its projectiles—you'll take a few hits—then fire Projectiles again when the demon descends. Repeat. Unfortunately, when the monster "dies," it becomes more powerful: armor collects around its remains, reanimating them. Stay on the left side as it reforms, and shoot Aura to weaken it. Your goal is to hit the monster's blue, beating Heart when it's exposed. When you can see it, low in its chest, move slightly left of center, firing Projectiles at it, pausing only to strike at the fireballs it flings at you.

Being a god isn't easy.

If, by the way, you want to play the game without having to build cities, wait until you've finished, go to the title screen, indicate New Game, and a third choice will appear: Special. Go to that and you won't see your winged buddy at all.

ating: A
> *Challenge:* A
>> You've got to use hand/eye coordination during the Act segments, and you've got to think and analyze during the Simulation interludes. What more could you ask for? Well—
>
> *Graphics:* A
>> How about incredible graphics? Excellent animation and detail in the Acts (the clouds in Aitos, Act I, will knock your eyes out!) and the building of the towns in Simulation—especially the scurrying people and animals—are terrific.
>
> *Sound Effects:* A

The musical score is glorious, and so are the sound effects.

Simulation: A

The characters are so deferential, and the illusion so complete, you'll feel like a mythological god!

DARIUS TWIN

Type: Space shoot-'em-up

Objective: A long time ago, the evil space barbarian Belser and his hordes invaded the peaceful planet Darius. Some Dariusites were able to escape to other worlds . . . and now, centuries later, their descendants in the Galactic Federation must prevent the wicked tyrant from claiming more worlds. To do this, you must board your Silver Hawk spaceship and attack Belser's outpost worlds and, finally, the despot's home base.

Heroes: Your ship can begin the game with up to eight lives (see note at bottom of *Strategies*), and you can arm it with a rapid-fire capability if you wish. There are sixteen different routes to Darius, and you can select variations—though all take you to similar worlds. Along the way, your Silver Hawk will be able to shoot packs of floating squares, which, when they're all defeated, release various power-up items— space combat armaments that range from shields to more powerful bombs and guns, which include multi-directional firing. Be careful: on planet surfaces, you can self-destruct by flying into the ground or against machinery. Also, be aware that when you die and get a new ship, you can't grab power-ups immediately: you've got to wait until your ship stops flashing—though you can fire the instant you reappear.

Enemies: Various spaceships and monsters, including moderately powered "Middle Bosses" and tough-to-beat "Final Bosses."

Menu: One or two players can soar simultaneously.

Scoring: Points are awarded for defeating enemies.

Strategies: In general, wherever possible, don't plug the last ship of any given power-up wave until you're relatively near to it. Otherwise, you may have trouble getting to the power-up as it drifts toward the bottom of the screen and other ships arrive. Also, your first order of business should be to buy yourself some manuevering room by destroying the ships in the center.

Planet Rilair: When the ground-based artillery shoots at you, move from the left to the center of the screen so you'll have room to duck and dodge the shells. After the first guns vanish, go to the left, under the score, and stay halfway up the screen: the ships dropping and rising at you will miss you and fly right into your sights. When the Middle Boss Dark Angel arrives, duck the first shockwave and go in the direction *opposite* the one in which the fish is moving. Otherwise you'll be cornered by the next two waves. When the Boss arrives—Killer Higia—drop to just above the waterline (roughly the same height as your ship is long, level with the monster's mouth), shooting constantly from the far left. All of the monster's projectiles will miss you or be shot down, while your shots will strike home.

Planet Danto: Stay to the far left, sweeping up and down and shooting away; the only time you'll need to move to the middle are when the small corallike ships arrive. They take multiple hits to destroy, and you can only get in enough of these if you're closer. When they're gone, go back to the left, but be prepared to rise or fall immediately when ships drop and rise from the far left. Take out the first two ships of the top or bottom phalanx at once, or they'll join with the other row and leave you no maneuvering room. When the Pente-Shark shows up, get right up against its nose and blast it. It'll spit out a single Shark which will become five and charge you. Back up and fire. Though you *can* slip through the quintet, you'd be wise to shoot at least one Shark to leave yourself a wide path through the onslaught. Note: any mini-Sharks launched before the Middle Boss dies will survive it and attack. There are two bosses—Emperor Fossil and Queen Fossil—one of which ejects little light beams, and the other big, fat ones, all of which are deadly. Only one boss opens its mouth at a time, which is good; remain on the far left and stay with the active fish, keeping up a steady fire while watching the projectiles coming toward you. *Hope* that your own projectiles hit, but don't watch the Big Boss: keep your eye on the indestructible beams coming at you, moving to the right—sometimes as far as the center and all the way to the bottom—while weaving to avoid them.

Planet Koloba: Familiar ships from Rilair, along with the coral vessels from Danto. The Pente-Shark and final bosses should be dealt with as above.

Planet Lankus: You need four-way projectiles in addition to your straight-ahead cannon to get through here. Stay just to the left of center so you'll not only be well-positioned to hit everything, but be able to move when the tunnels you're in start to shift around. As soon as you see the tips of red missiles on the bottom of the screen, go ahead of them or behind them: you don't want to be over them when they launch! When the Big Boss Demon Sword arrives from the top right, stay dead-center and dodge up and down slightly, without backing to the left, as projectiles spread out from the alien's top, then bottom, etc. Keep shooting at the monster's eyes until it dies.

Planet Padi: Stay just right of center, slightly toward the bottom, using four-way and forward shots simultaneously. Stay low when the big white projectiles come toward you, so you can destroy the ground-based gun that's shooting them, and dart to the right when giant Blowhards come at you from behind, then get in back of them and blast away. Dual Shears is the lobsterlike Big Boss. It arrives from the right: stay in the center, toward the top—it charges ahead now and then, so you can't stay in the middle—dropping down to fire at its head while ducking its projectiles (which aren't too fierce), and shooting its claws (which *are* fierce) when they detach. If you've got a lot of patience, just stay on the very top, out of the range of its fire or lunges, and just let your diagonal/right/down gun take care of it.

Planet Rear: More or less the same as the previous world. Stay slightly right of center, toward the bottom, to fend off creatures from right and left and the cannon in front. There's another Dual Shears at the end; fight it as described above.

Planet Narukini: They're coming at you steadily front and rear now. Stay dead-center, using all five directional guns. You'll have to go right to get behind some of the ships that come from that direction—especially the school of flying fish types that come in a bowling pin formation—since only your forward gun will really be effective against them. Go up, left slowly, then down when you're behind them—watching out for their rear-firing missiles. The Middle Boss, a Radiator Crab, is best dealt with by staying to its left, even with the antennae, and shooting ahead. The big squid-ships come singly, but there are several in succession, so get above or below and then behind them. The Big Boss is Dark Coronatus, a seahorse, and it comes from above, so start at the bottom left and move up when it arrives, firing repeatedly at its head and the tiny seahorses it ejects while avoiding (easily enough) its other projectiles.

Planet Karudo: Basically the same as above: stay toward the bottom center to pick off the missiles rising from below as well as the monsters that attack from the sides. Go left, center, to fight the Radiator Crab; when you've beaten it, stay dead-center, backing up to use your diagonal guns to hit the missiles from the bottom and swinging up and left to get behind the flying fish formations. When the Big Boss Dark Coronatus arrives, fight as described above.

Planet Sabia: Handle this planet mostly in the center bottom to start, then center after the first wave of flying fish arrive. Kill the three waves by going up, left, and behind—but only *after* the horizontal projectiles have been fired—kill the Radiator as before, get under the two squids, and stay low to fight all of the many land-based weapons. (You can't destroy the ones that spray out enemies like an exploding volcano, but you *can* kill the ejecta—so it's best to get *ahead* of these enemies as soon as they appear.) To fight the Big Boss, Red Mist, stay in the upper left—it arrives from bottom left—until it's in the center of the screen; then get in the center, to the right of its swinging tentacle, and shoot it from the opening that's spitting out projectiles. In case you haven't guessed it, Sabia is the toughest of the three planets you can choose at this juncture.

Planet Noeru: The screen scrolls diagonally, from the bottom right to the upper left; stay low in the center, easing to the left to blast those infernal red missiles as necessary. You want to stay to the right of the scrolling landscape wherever possible, lest you be pinned to the left side of the screen—and killed by the scrolling when you can't get around one of the floating pieces of landscape. The Big Boss is Full Metalshell. The turtle descends from the top center; stay in the upper left, blasting it diagonally, sweeping to the right when it comes left, and dropping down to shoot its face directly only when you're feeling brave. The tortoise spits out baby turtles, fires vertical projectiles, and extends its head now and then: stay on top or die!

Planet Harolain: The screen scrolls from the top right to the bottom left, so stay in the top left for the first half, then move to the center; you'll know when you need to do this!

The big pain here is the boss, Hyper Great-thing. It's going to come down from the top right; stay on the bottom left and shoot at the nose of the giant whale. When it moves to the top, get above it and blast the turrets on its back. When it comes to the top, get under it, orbit it to the right, and get on its left by crossing backwards over the top. Repeat as often as necessary.

Planet Darius: Stay in the upper left until the Radiator Crab arrives: you won't be touched by anything up there. After that you're on your own, darting and weaving as virtually all of the Middle Bosses charge you at once. If you get to the Big Boss Super Alloy-lantern, you probably won't need *our* help. But in case you do—get on the bottom left when it arrives and blast it where it's disgorging fish-things. After beating this monstrosity, you'll face the Great Tusk, the boss of bosses. Stay at the far left and shoot at its head—if you get the chance!

If you're having trouble getting through the game, the solution is, fortunately, a simple one. When you switch on the game, move the cursor to the number of players you want, then hold down the L and R buttons on controller two, then hold down the select button on controller one. Press start on controller one and you'll begin the game with a total of fifty ships!

Rating: B–

   Challenge: B

   There are some difficult passages, but you'll have so much firepower, it won't be much trouble getting through them. Only Darius is a real killer.

   Graphics: B

   There are some great visuals here, especially the cloudy graphics of Narukini. The bosses are well animated—particularly Red Mist—but the ships themselves are pretty uninspired.

   Sound Effects: C

   Standard music and explosions—good of that type, but there isn't much more.

   Simulation: C–

   Things come at you so quickly, and you've got to dart so often, you'll never *really* feel like you're flying.

D-FORCE

Type: Aerial shoot-'em-up

Objective: A mad Middle East tyrant has waged war on the world and, seated in your nuclear Apache Helicopter D-Force, you've got to fly through six countries and teach him a lesson.

Heroes: Your chopper can fly in all directions—including up and down in the Exploration mode—and comes equipped with a basic Cannon. As you destroy select foes, you uncover power-ups which boost your firepower in different ways.

Enemies: You'll face everything from Jets to Bombers to Helicopters to Dinosaurs (!) and Mythological Beasts (!!) as you fight your way to the dictator's lair.

Menu: You can play the game straight through or fight through the Shooting and Exploration modes separately.

Scoring: You earn points for every foe you down.

Strategies: What can you expect from the different stages of play? Funny you should ask. We'll take you through the first half of the game; after that, *only* rapid reflexes and a full arsenal of weapons will help.

Gulf Installation: After the first two waves of Fighters from the front, you'll get a wave of three weaving Fighters, followed by a big one coming at you from behind on the right—along with regular Fighters swooping in from the left. Concentrate on the big plane, getting under it and avoiding its backward Plasma fire. When it's destroyed, there'll be a wave of planes swooping in from the upper right, then another big Fighter on the left; make sure it doesn't "rear-end" you while you're going for the power-up left behind by the first. Helicopters come from the front, next, shooting at you; the last one will be on the right. When you destroy it, return to the center because a third Fighter will rise up from behind. Fortunately, all of the big Fighters will leave behind power-ups to give you more firepower. A trio of Bombers will fly at you from the front, fire, then retreat—unless you've bagged them, of course—and two more big Fighters will arrive simultaneously from behind. When you reach the shore, Fighters will take off in rows, left and right, to attack: polish off one at a time. A row of planes will soar in from the upper left and dive-bomb you, followed by more from the top, then two big Fighters from behind. The Fighters here will be firing long, green Laser Beams at you, and they're not as easy to avoid as the bullets. Stay on the bottom, one plane wide over from the life counter in the lower right, ready to move any way you must in order to attack.

The rest of the foes are rehashes until the end. Play on the bottom center of the screen so you'll have time to get all the waves coming from ahead and be able to shift left or right to get the ones rising from behind.

At the end of the level, circles of fire will rise from the woods, followed by a huge Fighter, the miniboss Electro Rocker. It will stay on the center top of the screen then charge down on the sides; battle it by moving in a large U-shaped motion from the top of one side, down to the center bottom, to the top of the other. Break off now and then to avoid its fire, then resume the pattern.

After defeating it, you'll find yourself over an Airstrip. Sweep back and forth on the bottom, toasting the Tanks, Trucks, and Turrets ahead. Very few come at you from behind, and those that do are easily picked off—especially if you've got Missiles coming out your side! This level's a turkey shoot until the boss Super Tank at the end—it arrives after you pass the six blocks of trees, three on either side. Super Tank occupies a good portion of the top half of the screen and throws everything at you, from projectiles to Laser Beams. If you've got side Missiles, go to the upper right and fire away. Move down slightly so you can hit the guns on the left from this vantage point: when you're tucked in the top right corner, the Tank can't get you. When the four Turrets are gone, stay in the corner and shoot Missiles at the Tank until it explodes. If you don't have Missiles, move back and forth along the bottom, and don't get close if you don't have to.

Inland Sector One: You'll be able to stay high to kill the Archeopteryxes there, but you'll have to drop down (left button) to get the lower protobirds as well as the Triceratopses—which fire at you—and the boss Dorf, a Tyrannosaurus. You can avoid the monster's swinging tail by placing yourself in the bottom left corner and simply firing at its head. Both head and tail explode when it dies.

Mirage Installation: Start in the center, just above the bottom of the screen, swinging left and right to blast the globular ships and darting to the center to avoid the crossfire. (If you want to avoid them altogether, just position yourself a plane's length above the bottom center. Their fire will miss you.) After they leave, another big Fighter rises from the bottom right, then one from the bottom left . . . the latter accompanied by Saucers that descend from the opposite side and then circle you, firing. Don't be tempted by the big Fighter: tackle the Saucers first by sliding all the way over to the right and taking them out as they swoop down from that side; if you fail to get them, try and stay in the center of the screen so you can weave around the fire coming from all directions. More Saucers attack from the left, next, along with a big Fighter. Again, destroy the Saucers first by sliding to the far left side of the Fighter and shooting them down. A slew of huge Missiles comes from the top left and right—easy to hit or avoid—followed by more Laser Beam firing ships as in the last, sent out from in-ground bases on the right, then left. Stay to the left of the life numbers as before. More Missiles, big Fighters, and Jets arrive; play them all by staying in the bottom center as much as possible. The exceptions are the green-nosed Jets, which dive-bomb you at the bottom; play to the sides and pick them off when they appear.

After this very busy round, you'll fight a bunch of Tanks on the left and right, and a few from behind after the ninth Tank up front, so don't stay too low on the screen—if you've got the Homing Missiles, they'll start firing backwards by themselves, tipping you off that the Tanks are coming. Fight the ones from behind on the right bottom, firing to the left; when these are gone, *stay* in the corner, shooting left to take out the three that rise up in turn. There will be two large

Tanks on either side up ahead of you: get under one, then the other. These will be followed by a pair of deadly Plasma Tanks. These two biggies will fire Plasma Balls like those spewed by the big Fighters. They're easy to beat: get in the far right corner and simply ride slightly up or down to avoid their fire while launching your own.

After that it's on to another Tank base like the one you fought in the first level . . . only a lot *busier!* Many of the Tanks here fire Homing Missiles of their own. Also, some Tanks don't show up until you're halfway up the screen, since they're pulling out of installations left and right. Play on the bottom to destroy what you can by shifting left and right; if you miss anything, pull up to the center to try and avoid their fire. After you get through this region, it's relatively clear sailing for a while—just two Tanks on either side—followed by a rehash of what you just suffered through.

The boss, the SR-72 plane, is a killer. It comes from below and not only fires circular projectiles, but also you-seeking Missiles! If you've got Homing Missiles, stay dead-center in the screen and circle its two kinds of projectiles—usually counterclockwise—to avoid them, using your own Missiles all the while. When the ship rises, get under it and blast away. If you haven't got Missiles, you've got to do the same thing —stay in the center and get under the SR-72 when you can—though you don't have the advantage of firing back while you're there!

Mythical East: There are two Catapults smack in front of you, hurling rocks, followed by fire-breathing Statues. Time your moves through them, watching out for more Catapults ahead, as well as additional Statues. If you want to drop down to avoid the Statues, go right ahead: but you'll face the more difficult-to-pass Arrow-firing Centaurs and the Sphinx Statues which come to life and attack. At the end you've got to go down and face the fire-breathing two-headed Gryphon: get in front of the right head, shoot at it, and avoid the fire from both heads by sliding to the right, going up, then cutting back down so you're in front of the head. You can destroy the left head by standing just to the right of its fireballs and shooting ahead: you won't have to dodge a thing!

Fantasy Icequarters: Stay in the center, close to the bottom, throughout: you'll need plenty of reaction time for the enemies attacking from above. Your reflexes are the *only* thing that's going to help you get through here.

Inland Sector Two: The ship comes from behind you here, firing diagonally, so your inclination is to drop down. The thing is, you can only fly between the buildings. So before you drop, get a look at an area where there's lots of room up ahead. Ships waiting below will attack, but they're not as tough as the one up above! Beware, though: when you rise, you may fly right up into the ship and be destroyed. If you opt to stay up in the air, you can ride up and down the far left or right side to avoid the giant ships' projectiles, particularly in the lower corners. The boss is easy to beat: drop down to fire, rise to avoid its fire, then drop down again. Your targets are the main Turrets straight ahead, the Cannons on the side, and the Turrets in the back.

Throughout the rest of the game there are safe zones for most bosses—that is, you won't get clobbered from all sides at once—and you should seek these out: most are in the corners, with some jockeying up and down required.

Unfortunately, there is no way to execute level select. Or to save your game. Lose, and you've got to fly through the previous levels all over again.

A word to Asmik: there are lots of typos in the instruction booklet—ulimate, dinasaurs, loosing instead of losing, etc. One reader, Chris Kern, took us to task for criticizing game manufacturers for typos while we make some ourselves in our books. That's true. Out of 60,000 words, we blow one or two. We *try* not to, but it happens. Unfortunately, too many game companies don't even make the effort. To miss three or more words out of a few *hundred* simply isn't acceptable. It's unprofessional *and* it gives ammunition to antivideogame factions that feel the games are bad for us! The problem isn't only with homegrown games: with translations by and from the Japanese becoming more and more commonplace, the problem will worsen if it isn't dealt with *now*.

Rating: B–

Challenge: A

You'll be kept on your toes from the word go!

Graphics: C+

Some very good visuals in the Exploration mode, but the Shooting mode isn't as exciting.

Sound Effects: C

Nothing exceptional explosion or music-wise; the helicopter's cannon sounds are good.

Simulation: C+

You'll feel as though you're airborne now and then, though not as much as you might like.

DRAKKHEN

Type: Fantasy quest

Objective: The wicked Dragons are the masters of the four elemental forces: earth, water, air, and fire. As if that weren't enough, the hateful Dragons have stolen the eight Tears of Drakkhen Island, the jewels that represent all the powers of magic. Guess who's got to get them back? Your journey will cover three realms: Ice, Marsh, Forest, and Desert.

Heroes: You control a party consisting of four warriors who start out with a limited amount of experience, magic, and weaponry. They accumulate strength as you prosecute your adventure—specifically, strength (HP, for hit points), weapons, and magic (MP). They also collect Jade, which allows them to purchase weapons and magic from wandering Merchants. The warriors have access to a map/compass screen to chart their journey. Outside the Dungeons—which are actually Castles—players can almost always cause monsters to run by pressing the left and right buttons alternately and quickly . . . though the monsters may get in a hit or two. If you choose to fight, the NES controls the actual battle: you just sit there and watch!

Important note: the instructions aren't terribly clear about this, but once you take a weapon, it just sits in your arsenal until you put it on! To do so, activate the character icon—upper left of the lower right screen—go to "weapons," access "equipment," and move the cursor to the newly acquired weapon. You can replace old equipment with stronger versions by repeating the process. Each character can only carry a certain number of weapons; you can, however, give equipment to other members of your party if you want to acquire something new. Make sure you arm yourself with a more powerful weapon as *soon* as you acquire it. There are also two Warp stations, one located in the far west/center, just north of the border between Forest and Marsh; and one in the far east, directly north of the eastmost Inn of the three in the Marsh. Teleportation magic is useful here.

Finally, scattered throughout the map are Anak installations where you can go to be healed: even the dead can be raised—assuming at least one member of your party is still alive. Anak wizards will restore your hit points (HP) to the highest level they'd achieved during the game, and you'll still have any weapons you had when you died . . . although weapons you lost prior to your death will not be returned to you.

Note: you can separate warriors from the group and have them explore on their own, and you can create your own characters if you wish. Also, Hermes and Merlin will get the Unlock power; when they both have it, always use Hermes to Unlock doors. You'll want to save Merlin's strength for Anti-Matter and other offensive weapons. Finally, even if you're in the midst of battle, you can't be hurt while you're on the character or weapon symbol of the icon screen. That means you can switch weapons in the middle of battle. However, you *can* be attacked when you go to the icon screen to save your game . . . except, obviously, if the game is in the process of being saved.

Enemies: As if your search weren't difficult enough, scattered throughout the realm are forces loyal to you . . . but many more that are loyal to the Dragons. These include Mummies, Snakes and Scorpions—they're poisonous, so use "Cure" quickly—Centaurs, Bats, giants, giant spiders, giant alligators, and even giant giants, some of which rise from the ground, others that descend from the skies, some simply dropping, others forming from constellations before coming at you. The ones you definitely want to avoid are the Dragons at the Flickering Lights in the center of the screen and in the Desert. You can talk to them while you have limited power, but once you're powered-up they'll attack you mercilessly. Most enemies give you Jade when they perish, especially those you slay in the various Castles—called Dungeons, though they aren't really. Watch out for the water—you'll lose HP as you waddle out—even if you aren't in the water when you're just viewing the terrain ("invisible," so to speak), your people may end up in the water when they become visible to do battle. Also beware the little statues that litter the terrain: bump into one and a giant deadly Cat-thing will appear, roaring like the Id Monster from *Forbidden Planet*. So . . . when you see these things at the crossroads and elsewhere, avoid them!

Menu: There is only the one quest, although the cartridge has the capacity to save two separate games.

Scoring: No points: just Jade and greater power.

Strategies: Important: save the game often, especially after you acquire a powerful new weapon or item, or reach a new level of experience. You can't save games inside Castles, so to make sure you don't lose something terrific you've just acquired, it's a good idea to hit the doorway icon, which whisks you outside the Castle, and save the game . . . then make your way back to where you were. (Better to do that than to feel like a dork if you get great stuff, haven't saved the game, then run into a monster that kills two of your party.)

Begin by entering Prince Hordkhen's Castle straight ahead. Take the Buckler from the wall on the right, then touch the second symbol from the left to eliminate the energy barrier. (If you want to try and gain HP, hit the other symbols and fight monsters. Just keep an eye on your HP: it's easy to die when they're this low!) When the force field is down, enter the door on the top left, go right and walk *through* the tapestry. Take the Short Swords from the wall and arm your crew. Return to the first room and go left, then left again. Talk to the Old Man, then go back to the first room and head up the main staircase. Fight the monster here if you want, go left, then go left again . . . fighting the monster in this room. Exit front/bottom and have a chat with Prince Hordkhen. He'll send you on a mission to see his sister Princess Hordkha; hit the doorway icon and save the game outside the Castle.

Head northeast. You'll hit the Flickering Lights; follow them, with the lights to your right. Go around them when they end, but do *not* head into the Marsh: you have to be powered-up to go there. (Don't worry: an Old Man will warn you back.) When you're around them, head southeast to Anak for cures, then travel due east to the Castle. Get the message there, then return to the castle of Prince Hordkhen and give him the bad news. On the way back, engage in battles as you near Anak: you'll need to acquire more power, especially the skill of Unlock, which Merlin usually gets first. Heal up at Anak, then it's back to Hordkhen.

Watch out for the Shark that's suddenly appeared in the Moat: cross the drawbridge *only* the instant the Shark appears on the right side of it. Otherwise, you're fish food. Inside, have someone take the Buckler off the wall, do some fighting by pressing the "wrong" symbols if you want—if you've saved the game outside the Castle, you can restart the game if you get too badly beaten up; there's nothing to lose and a lot of weapons and Jade to gain! When you're done here, go up one room, then use Unlock to enter the door on the right. Nothing in here, but go through the door foreground/right. Slay the monster in here— a pretty powerful one, which is why you should've done some fighting in the "foyer"—and stand on the symbols in turn. Then use "touch" on the skull chest in the middle. Doors will open elsewhere and will be used in good time. Don't go to the left—mean Scorpion inside, and aught to gain—but return to see the Prince. He'll tell you where to find his sister: in Haaggkhen's Castle, in the north Swamp. He makes your bodies strong enough to enter that region now. However, before you go, slip past him and enter the room on the right—remember the skull chest you touched? Take the Light Greave and Light Cuirass from the wall on the right—use "touch" twice. Take the Key from the right Bookcase. Go down, then down—going right instead leads to dead-end rooms: you've got to open a door before going here. There's a pool: go down one more time. Step on the Grate to open a door "somewhere." Take the two Torches from this room, then go up, up again, right—avoid the Grate, which unleashes a Scorpion—then down. The door you opened is in the foreground/right. Enter, read the Coffins, go down again. Fight the onslaught of monsters, power yourself up, then use the doorway icon. Head northwest, carefully crossing the road that leads across the Swamp. (Remember: falling in the water will cost you HP.)

Upon arriving at the Castle of the Water Prince Haaggkhen, use Unlock to open the Castle door, then hit the rightmost symbol to eliminate the energy field —or press the other symbols to fight monsters, if you're up for it. Go in the doorway ahead, Unlock the one in the next room and go ahead, then head left in the next chamber. Light up the room and exit through either top door right: kill the monster and get the Shields. Then go back down and head through the left door. Move through here quickly, so you don't have to fight the Bat, exiting through the draped door on top. Go left, then down, then left. Go up: take the Heavy Shield from the wall. Go down, down either door, and use Unlock to open the door at the bottom. Avoid the monster in the Fireplace: if you kill it, a succession of Flame Creatures will arrive to trouble you. Go down again, only this time kill the creature Fireplace and go over to it. Throw a lever, and a door will open "somewhere." Exit on the right. Go down, kill the Rats, and Unlock the door on the right. Enter and go down. You're in the pool room: go down, but avoid the Coffin in the next room. It'll unleash a succession of tough-to-kill Witch creatures. Go right and enter another pool room. Go to the pool and then isolate your strongest warrior (blue dot) and put him/her in the left side of the Pool. Look at the waters and he/she will be teleported to a water room in which the only exit is on the left. Not only will the water weaken you, but a water monster will attack—and if you kill it, another will arrive—so it's advisable to get out quickly! When you exit the water room on the left, you'll find yourself in a jail. Talk to the prisoner. (If you don't have light magic here, one of the characters you left behind can use it: you'll still be able to see.)

When you release the Prisoner, you'll be told where to go next. If you exit left, down, and down, you and your party will escape the Castle. Good idea: do so and save your game. Then reenter, kick some monster butt for power, and go up. In the room above the entranceway, go up after using Unlock—left will bring you to monster rooms and back to the foyer— head left, go up right to fight the monster and get more Shields, go down again and up the left door- way, head past the Bat and go through the Drapes, then go left, down, left, and up to take the Heavy Shield—if you have someone who can carry it. Hit doorway on the icon chart and leave.

Go northeast to the Castle, get your "permit"— really just a chat with the occupant—and go to Prin- cess Naakhtkha's Castle in the northwest. (The Ice Inns here are a waste of time.) Once inside, hit the symbol to the immediate right of the door to elimi- nate the force field—or press the others to fight for power-ups. Go up and use Unlock to go right. Kill the monster and collect the weapons and armor inside. Exit down and either fight or avoid the monster: go right and face the fiend within, arming Hestia and Merlin with magic, and the other two with weapons. You'll get 1000+ Jade. Exit left and kill the monster now; exit the Castle and save what you've got, then reenter. Shut off the energy field, go up, go up again —don't go left: the door will lock behind you—Un- lock the door on the right, listen to the Old Man, head up, fight the monster or just scurry up, touch the two switches in back to unlock doors "somewhere," then go back to the room above the entrance—where you met the monster and first Unlocked the doors. Go right, down, right, down, left (Unlock), down (Un- lock), down, and you'll be at a Bath. Unlock and go right: enter the door below the Coffin—which has nothing of value to you, so don't waste Light—go down, down again, and right (Unlock). You'll find Princess Hordkha there. She'll give you your first Tear and tell you to hie to the Palace of Water Princess Haaggkha. If you want to do more exploring in the Castle for Jade and such, enter, eliminate the energy field, Unlock the door and go up, go up, right, up, up again—pulling the switches—left, left again (Unlock), up through the curtain and slay the monster if you wish. Go left: read the Books inside, head up through the drapes, and go right into the Princess's room. Take the Lucky Staff on the right. Go up, read the message ahead of you, then go through the door on the right. Kill the occupant and exit the castle.

Head southwest, stopping at Anak. Fight everything you meet, saving often: unless you lose a major piece of equipment—in which case, reset the game—you can have it restored at Anak. From there, head southeast to the castle. (This, by the way, is a great place to collect Jade: press the left symbol and you'll get around 1000, usually more, each time you slay a monster. And all you have to do to save them is step out the door, save, and reenter.) Hitting the symbol on the right, head up then up again, then again. Go left, up, up through either door, then left. Have a chat with Princess Haaggkha. She'll send you back to destroy the turncoat Hordkhen at his abode and, Ozlike, order you to return with his Tear . . . so it's back to the southwest and the Castle to the left of the Flickering Lights in the Forest.

Inside the Castle of Prince Hordkhen, use only Weapons (no Magic) until you face the fiend. You'll need to be fully charged. Repeat the drill as before—first going to the room with the Skull Chest and opening the distant door—visiting the Prince: only this time, he's going to attack with fury! If you haven't got enough power, collect Jade, buy arms, and wait until you're strong enough. If you've got War Rings and Ghost Staff, those are useful. Beat the Prince and you've got your second Tear. Make sure you power-up in the room behind him once you've been decimated.

When you're finished here, it's back to the Castle in the Swamp. (Don't get cocky after defeating the Prince: on the road, Centaurs can still whip you!) It's a good idea to spend some time killing the guard monsters inside the doorway: they give a lot more Jade than those at the Castle you just left, and you'll need the wealth and weapons—and if you get beaten . . . just reset again! And it's okay to use Magic to slay them: you'll have enough time on the road to recharge. At your audience with her highness, Haaggkha will give you your third Tear and send you to find out why the Fire Princess Hazhulkha hasn't been heard from. You'll have to journey to her Castle in the southwest. Unfortunately, the only way to get inside is exactly at dawn. Otherwise, there's no entry. You also learn you're supposed to meet Prince Naakhtkhen in the desert. But you're not finished here! Use the doorway icon to leave, save your game, then reenter. Go up, then *right*. You'll find yourself in the Unicorn room. Don't bother with the horse: go down (Unlock), right (Unlock), down either door—after reading the Book in the very *center* of the Bookcase . . . and not worrying about the monster, which will run away—down, down (right is a monster room), right, down, right, down (Unlock), down (the monster won't hurt you), down, right, down (Unlock), and right (Unlock). Inside is a powerful monster. Talk to it and it'll attack. When it's defeated—and you're 2000+ Jade richer . . . assuming you've used some heavy duty items—go right. Go down (Unlock), then adjust the four Buttons so they read

4281. Fight the Dragon in the next room—a killer reptile which'll cost you dearly—then go down and restock your weapons. Use the doorway icon and leave.

The Desert's a dangerous place, with most of the menaces being the toughies from the skies. So travel through the Forest as much as possible, then cut down to the Castle. If you get there and it's not dawn, hang around: your window of opportunity is slight! (Save the game as the sky begins to brighten: if you blow it, you can reset and try again!)

Inside, take any door. Go right, up—there's nothing to the right—left, left (Unlock), down, left, up, left, up, right, right, down either door, and feast your eyes on the dead Princess Hazhulkha. Go down (Unlock) and kill the monster and Prince Naakhtkhen will arrive. Talk to him and he'll give you another Tear after telling you to go to the Castle of Naakhtkha and kill her. So . . . it's back to the northwest Ice Castle to kill the Princess.

Back at the Castle, get rid of the energy barrier then enter. Unlock and go up, then up again through either door, then right (Unlock), up, up (hit the Switches here), left, left (Unlock), up, up, and fight the Princess. You'll get 8000+ Jade, a Tear . . . and Prince Naakhtkhen will show up—after the job is done, natch. You'll get another Tear from him and he'll tell you to take Prince Haaggkhen's gem from him. Then Prince Hazhulkhen's after that.

You've got six Tears now: head back to the castle in the western Marsh. Enter and go up, up, up on the left, up through the drape, left, down, left, and up. When you face the Prince, you'll need more power than you've ever used before.

Winning your seventh Tear, pay visits to the two Tents in the south—east, then west—to get your "permit," then go to the last Castle: the court of the Prince of Fire and Death, Hazhulkhen. The symbol to the immediate left of the door will kill the energy field. If you want to get some Dragon-level armaments, go up, left, down, left, down (Unlock)—the monster here won't hurt you—and left. Listen to the Old Man in here and go down (Unlock). Go left, down (Unlock), right, down, down (Unlock), down (Unlock), right, down (Unlock), and grab any armor you need. Exit using the doorway icon.

Go back in, de-energize the force field, go left, up (Unlock), left, up (Unlock), and left. Go up (Unlock), right, up, and left (Unlock). Kill the monster here— 2000+ Jade plus a weapon—and go left (Unlock) to fight another monster. Head up and light the room. Take the stairs up. Unlock and go up to visit the Prince. Kill him and get the last Tear. When Hazhulkhen dies, the Priest of the Plains Shrine appears. He sends you on a final mission to the Island's Center to "convert the eight gems to the ninth Tear."

Don't expect any of the island monsters to give you a break: they'll all still attack as you make your way northwest. At the northern edge of the Flickering Lights, four Dragons will come and greet you, congratulate you, and give you the moral of the tale. They'll also tell you that another challenge awaits you —meaning you should design your own team and start again.

Rating: B–
> *Challenge:* B–
> Very interesting, and at times puzzling, though once you get powered-up, things get a little dreary. The game might have been somewhat more exciting if there were more to do or look at in the Dungeons.
> *Graphics:* B–
> Good animation and scenery, especially when you teleport. There's occasional image breakup

when too many moving characters are on the screen. The Warp graphics are exciting.

Sound Effects: C+

Good music, but only fair monster voices.

Simulation: B

You'll often feel like you're actually in the adventure . . . though the fact that you sit out the fighting after you've chosen the weapons is frustrating.

JOE KOVIN

sweeps too many missing clues aus along on the
arrears. The Narrow—space
Goldsmith rarer's
late
out the
Before the x speed
As rate

FINAL FIGHT

Type: Wrestling and martial arts quest

Objective: Metro City's in sorry shape. The city lives in
fear of the Mad Gear Gang, but Mayor Mike Haggar
has vowed to destroy them. To scare him off, the
gangsters grab his daughter Jessica; but Mayor Haggar doesn't know the meaning of retreat. Drawing on
his own wrestling experience, he goes after the gang
personally. Also out to destroy the thugs is Jessica's
boyfriend Cody, a master of martial arts.

Heroes: Haggar and Cody can walk in any direction and
use various holds, throws, kicks, and punches to fell
their foes. As they bash their way through Metro City,
they can replenish their Strength Meters by feasting
on various foods that can be obtained by smashing
various crates, barrels, etc. Weapons are also hidden
around the city.

Enemies: Sundry lowlife gang members and their powerful bosses. The longer you take to get rid of them, the
more they'll gather and gang up on you! If enemies *do*
collect, you can hurt them by throwing or knocking
them into one another. Some thugs carry weapons, so

concentrate on getting rid of these guys first—and quickly!—even if you have to take a few knocks from the others.

Menu: One player plays alone as Mike or Cody. You can switch characters during the game's "continue" mode.

Scoring: In addition to beating enemies, points are awarded by picking up various items. You are also playing against a clock, which ticks down as you make your way through various sections of the city. The clock restarts each time you die.

Strategies: In general, as you fight, you should position yourself in the middle of the screen so you'll have some room to move if you need to retreat. The exceptions are discussed below. Also, try to push crowds of enemies off the right side of the screen. A lot of them can't somersault back on, and if you keep up a barrage of hits, you'll spare yourself a lot of damage—if they aren't onscreen, they can't hurt you . . . but you can hurt them. This works especially well in the Bay Area as you near the Statue of Liberty.

Regarding food, expose it but don't necessarily eat it right away. If it restores all your energy, why not wait until you really need it? Get in as many hits as you can, wait till your strength meter is low, then replenish it.

Here's the level-by-level lowdown:

Slum: The first area is simple: you'll get food from the Tires if you need it, a bonus-point item from the Drum, and another from the next Drum. In the second area there are two Crates to smash. In the third section there's food in the Tires. When you face Thrasher —who bursts unexpectedly from the door—stay to the left. When he gets weak, he sits out the fighting and lets proxies handle it, so make sure you are in good shape, energywise. Hit one of the thugs with a Knife: you can claim it and put it to good use.

Subway: Break both Barrels for a weapon and item in the first section. You may find a Sword there, which will really let you make hash of your opponents. Inside the subway train, break both Barrels for items. At the end of the car you'll find where there are the third and fourth Barrels—break them and make your stand on the right: the end of the car will protect one of your sides. Next section: the Drum on the left always has Roast Beef. Put the fence to your back (on the right) at the end of the section. When you face the boss, Katana, approach along the near rope, come at him along the side, and hit him to the left. He'll usually drop his Sword; pick it up and stay pressed to the far rope, in his corner, so he has to come to you. Hit him when he does, and then stay with him, hitting and kicking relentlessly. If you manage to get both his Swords from him, keep him from the other one, which'll remain on the ground.

During the bonus round, pick up the Pipe in the foreground to smash the car.

Westside: Nothing unexpected in the first phase. In the bar there are a lot of thugs, but you can deal with that. With the twins, get the Sword, stay toward the left and keep hacking at them as they charge from the right. In the next section get the food from the Drum. When you run up against the Blutolike boss Edi-E, hit him first and stay close to him in the early going, getting in your hits. When he knocks you away, go on his right side and stay there as much as possible, using that side of the screen to protect your back. If you die, you'll come back on the left, so be prepared to

JEFF ROVIN

make your way over. Also, Edi-E starts to shoot at
you after a while. Stay toward the foreground or
background as much as possible; that way, you can
move toward the screen or away from it to get out of
his line of fire.

Bay Area: Break all Drums to get food and items, and
be ready to face the brawny dudes at the dock. No
special tactics here: either you've got the strength to
beat 'em or you haven't. Some tips, though. After you
pass the first dog, be prepared for a heavy duty assault from Wong Who, G. Oriber, and Bill Bull. Don't
nestle yourself in the left or right corner until they're
all on the screen. Only *then* can you use the corner for
protection. After that, watch out for the rolling
Drums. There are two sets, and if you don't bust them
up—and get what's inside—they'll run you down.
When you reach the second dog, stay in the front of
the screen and face left or right once the two Billys
and Sid have come along. In the rest room you'll face
a pair of Slashes: go to the right, but not *all* the way
over, since another Slash, some J's, and other thugs
will still be coming at you from that direction. Break
the Tires outside the lavatory, then be prepared to
face a trio of flamethrowers. If you kill the first one
before he can torch you, the others won't hurt you.
After this there are more Billys, Slash, etc. When you
face Abigail, hurt the bruiser by tossing flunkies into
him. (Yes, it's a him. Don't ask why.) Stay behind Abigail as much as possible; otherwise, you'll get
grabbed and flung, costing you half a strength meter's
worth of energy when you land. If you *are* caught,
Haggar's Super Spin and Cody's Super Kick will usually break you free . . . assuming you've got enough
energy to use them!

Break the glass in the bonus round by hitting them

48

smack in the middle and getting as close-in as possible to get more than one at once.

Uptown: The journey is longer and the foes are tougher here, and watch out as you go into the hotel: the Chandeliers aren't exactly *stable*. Watch the shadows on the floor to see where and when one's going to fall. (And collect the food from the first one!) Chandeliers aren't all that's dropping: in this level foes also fall from the ceiling. There's no warning, so be on your guard. By the time you get to the leader of the pack, you'll be surprised to find that he isn't as tough as Edi-E and Abigail . . . but he's surrounded by thugs, which makes the final fight particularly difficult. Hit Belger to free Jessica, then bash him repeatedly when you can. Break off your attack only when flunkies are plentiful and you have to deal with them.

Finally, if you want a real advantage when playing the game, go to a hidden menu by holding down the L and R keys and hitting start. You'll be able to make all kinds of changes in the game, including difficulty level and the number of lives you have.

.ating: A
> *Challenge:* A–
>> Though not *quite* as exciting as the arcade version, it's as close as a home game is likely to get. The fighters are diverse and the bosses are tough.
> *Graphics:* A–
>> Very fine animation and a minimal amount of image breakup. The sense of depth is particularly effective inside the subway car and right before the confrontation with Edi-E.
> *Sound Effects:* A
>> Excellent punching sounds, and the subway sounds are super-realistic.

Simulation: B–

There's no way that pushing a button's going to make you feel like you're throwing a punch or swinging a sword . . . but the game does as good a job as possible.

F-ZERO

Type: Racing game

Objective: It's nearly 600 years in the future, and people want new entertainment thrills. Hence, some genius came up with a Grand Prix race using floating, superfast bumper cars! There are seven different courses, each one more challenging—and deadly!—than the one before.

Heroes: Your vehicle can do everything but recite poetry. It can steer in any direction, accelerate, brake, move left or right, and butt other vehicles off the course. You have a choice of several vehicles which have different strengths and weaknesses. Each vehicle has a limited amount of energy which can be sapped by various obstacles. The courses afford occasional Jump Plates that briefly send you skyward. You can't move on to the next race unless you finish first, second, or third. A couple of hints about operating your machine. First, when you see someone coming up behind you, use the R and L buttons to get right in front. When you're nudged, you won't go flying off to the side but will get bumped ahead, *gaining* ground on your eager foe! Second, when you encounter Magnets, press down to help counteract their pull.

Enemies: In addition to the other racers, you have to face the Roughs along the sides of the courses, which slow you down; power-sapping Anti-Gravity Guide Beams that line the route—and force you to stay on the track; Mines; Magnets; and Dash Zones, which give you an unwanted burst of speed.

Menu: You can select the "Class" or difficulty level (Beginner, Standard, Expert) and League (Knight, Queen, or King)—that is, the level of course you wish to race. There's also a secret class that is not on the menu. If you play in the Expert Class mode, and finish first, second, or third in the five races of any league, you'll be able to play in a higher, more daunting Master Class. Check out the Select screen after your fifth victory.

Scoring: The farther you progress, the more points you win. Your progress also earns you a rank on the current course: you must finish the course at that rank or higher to be allowed to continue.

Strategies: The instruction booklet gives you the lowdown on all the vehicles; try them all and use the one which suits you best. Beginners find that the durable Fire Stingray or Wild Goose give them a feel for the game; experienced players will want to go with the faster but less sturdy Blue Falcon or the Golden Fox. Frankly, *we* recommend Fire Stingray for all players. It corners the best of all the vehicles, and while you may not *win* every course, you can certainly finish first, second, or third.

Here is the lowdown on the courses in each of the Leagues:

Knight League:

The tracks are fairly wide and there are few obstacles. Here's a track-by-track rundown.

Mute City I: Eight elbow turns, a few of them pretty tight, but there are also two long straightaways where you can pick up ground. Just one Jump Plate.

Big Blue: You're over water—which means, natch, there's some ice on the course. While there are only six elbow curves, there's a big area where, if you don't hug the inside of the track closely, you'll end up covering a wide area, wasting time.

Sand Ocean: Three tricky spots: a big C curve right after you begin, an extremely tight U curve nearly at the midway point, followed by a wriggly W. Open up after the W, taking the next long curves tight, hugging the center of the course, and really tear out on the straightaway next to the Pit Zone.

Death Wind 1: Heavy winds blow against you, so don't leave the middle of the course. At least the thing's a big O; on the Rough, use Super Jet to keep from losing time, while use the Dash Zone on the opposite side of the track to accelerate.

Silence: Early section is easy; when you come to the V area, the right side is longer, the left track shorter. But the left side leads through a field of Land Mines. Stay in the middle of the track: even if you go through it slowly, you'll save time. After you pass the Rough, you'll turn, come to another Rough, then enter a series of sharp curves. You can speed through the early ones if you're in the middle of the road; the last of them—in an S shape—have to be taken more slowly.

There's a long Rough, then another set of curves, which you should take slowly.

Queen League:

The tracks are narrower and there are more obstacles as you move from course to course.

Mute City II: After some easy going on mild Roughs, you'll come to an O section; no time saved whether you go left or right. Hug the inside whichever way you go and base your route on whichever is the least crowded—or most crowded, if you want to nudge some of your competition. Immediately after that you'll come to a Jump Plate followed by another: hit 'em hard and you'll gain some ground in these curves.

Port Town I: Go to the right side as soon as you start: there's a Jump Plate coming up and you'll certainly want it to leap over the break in the track up ahead. There's a soft U curve followed by a tight W in that order; when you get through those, Magnets will tug at you. Be ready to use the R and L buttons to pull yourself in the opposite direction.

Red Canyon I: The course is shaped more or less like a giant power-up Mushroom from *Super Mario World*! No real trouble here, but you've got a choice: to use the three Jump Plates in a row, or not. If you do, Magnets will pull you down. If you don't, you won't have to worry about that. The time spent both ways is roughly equal; base your judgment on (1) your personal skills, and (2) what your opponents are doing. Can you butt them when they come down from a Jump? Will they hit you if *you* Jump? Remember to press down for help against the Magnets. Shortly after this section you'll come to a wavy region, like a series of W's: stay in the middle and you'll have no trouble zipping through.

White Land I: The track is covered with ice, so in addition to cutting the corners close to the inside, slow down when you go into them. There's a long series of Jump Plates interspersed with Magnets; again, pressing down will help you to counteract the Magnets.

White Land II: More ice with a *lot* of curves; stay inside and be ready to slow down. There's also a huge break in the track, so be prepared for a major Jump!

King League:

Except for the first, this is a merciless series of tracks: there isn't a moment when you can coast or take a breather.

Mute City III: You'll start out with narrow but straight runs, then hit a major Rough stretch followed by two serious problem areas: a straightaway from which large, jagged bites have been taken from the sides. Stay in the middle here and just weave a bit left and right. After the next Rough, you'll turn into an insane stretch of Mines: best to use Super Jet here. If you slow down and pick your way through, you'll never finish in time. Otherwise, this isn't too bad a course.

Death Wind II: Hit the ground running and weave gently around the Roughs. After coming out of the U curve ahead, you'll hit Dash Zones: slow down or you'll spin madly ahead. After taking the next U curve, pour on the juice: there's nothing but clear road between you and the end.

Port Town II: You'll face the same gap as before, so

start on the right side; after that, there's a W curve followed at once by Magnets. Clear these and, except for the narrow track, you've got smooth sailing ahead.

Red Canyon II: Clear road until the Jump Plate/Magnet combination. Use the Jump Plates here: you'll want to use them to get over the jagged roadway ahead. Use your anti-Magnet moves and you'll be all right. You'll also want to hit the last Jump Plate and leap the gap that runs parallel to the track: if you stay on the road, the Mine field will kill you. When you clear this and turn to the right, stay in the center of the jagged road and Super Jet through.

Fire Field: You'll find yourself racing right into a Mine field. When you clear the last Mine, cut *at once* to the inside to swing around the very tight curve, open up a bit, negotiate the extremely tight U curve, then weave through the Roughs. Tear out ahead, staying to the inside—especially when you enter the U section in which the left side is all Rough. After you round a rather *hot* curve, the road divides. Doesn't matter which fork you take, but watch out for the powerful Magnet in the middle. When you get through here, time will be *very* important. So: hug the inside of the track—slow down a bit if you have to—and take the curve that turns *down* instead of the one that goes right. If you take the latter route, you won't win.

Rating: B

Before getting into specifics—and sorry to sound like a broken record here—while we all make typographical errors, the big, bold *biginner* on the bottom left of page seven in the instruction booklet is pretty embarrassing.

> *Challenge:* B+
>
> You won't find too many games that tax your

reflexes more. If you like racing games, they don't come any niftier.

Graphics: B+

Very good animation, excellent scenery.

Sound Effects: C+

Good racing and crashing effects, but the redundant music's gotta go!

Simulation: A

You'll feel every leap, turn, and crash!

GRADIUS III

Type: Space shoot-'em-up

Objective: It's a sad, familiar tale. You're a Gradiusan, and you've learned about Bacterion, a mass that's the source of evil in the universe. Like denizens of Gradius before you, you realize it's your duty to free oppressed worlds . . . which means that you must attack the issue of Bacterion in its many nefarious forms.

Heroes: Your M.A.X. starship can move in any direction and can be equipped with a variety of weapons, all of which are outlined in the instruction booklet. When waves of enemy ships are entirely destroyed, they leave behind power-ups which you must fly over to collect. Blue ones destroy virtually every enemy on the screen—though *not*, for example, Dragons in Zone One or Bubbles in Zone Two, and not projectiles. When Blue power-ups destroy ships, those ships leave behind any power-ups they were carrying. The appearance of Blue power-ups is entirely random; ships that give them in one game won't necessarily do so in the next. If you die, you're reborn more or less where you perished and not back at the beginning of the zone.

Enemies: The three basic varieties of foes are spaceships, monsters, and gun Turrets—some of which are stationary (Cankerzores) and some of which are robotic and move left and right around the terrain (Bazooka Heads). These are pictured in the instruction booklet. The terrain is also an enemy: if you hit it, you perish.

Menu: Two players can battle the enemy one at a time in alternating games.

Scoring: You earn points for every enemy you destroy.

Strategies: Here's the level by level strategy:

Zone One: Just waves of ships, top and bottom, until you reach the Dunes; the only surprise is a ship that attacks from the rear right before you reach the Dunes. Enter the Dunes firing at the top, get the Turrets there, then watch for them top and bottom. A Serpentine will rise up on the right and curl back at your ship. Stay left and shoot its head until it explodes. (If you miss it, it'll leave the sand, circle off the left of the screen, and come back at you.) Watch out for the battery of Turrets on top after that, followed by several on the bottom and then a narrowing of the Dune tunnel. Stay halfway between left and center, in the vertical center of the screen, and let the ships come to you here. Another Serpentine follows: though it, too, rises from the bottom, you'll have to let it get a little closer than the last one, since there's some landscape on top between you and the monster's vulnerable head. The Tunnel widens . . . but then a third Serpentine rises from the ground just left of center. Stay to the far left and blast it before it attacks. The boss, the Earwig Scorpion, comes from the end of the Tunnel on the right; it's only vulnerable when its pincers are open. Stay to the far left, middle of the screen, and fire ahead at the monster and the projectiles that come from its mouth. Move slightly to the right and down or up when its monster aides come from the top and bottom on the left; if you haven't got Shields or anything but straight-ahead guns, blast as many of the creatures as you can and simply avoid the rest; they'll go offscreen and won't return. When the monster's fireballs split—when you hit them or when they explode of their own volition—simply maneuver around them.

Zone Two: Waves of spaceships come at you quicker here; after the vertical-line formation, you'll enter the Carbonation Zone cavern. Take out the Turrets on top then shift quickly to the ones that follow, on the bottom. The big Bubbles ahead break up into deadly pieces when hit; take them all out as you would a V-shaped squadron of fighters. (Or avoid them: they won't attack, and if you don't hit 'em, they won't break up.) Watch for the Turret disgorging ships on the top and, after weaving through the first onslaught of Bubbles, stay close to the top: when you see the open pit up there, get to the left and start firing. Bubble Mites will emerge; you've got to pop the Bubble and *then* kill the Mite inside. Stay on the top and kill the first two this way; go around the rest and hit the Turrets on top for power-ups if you need them. Above all, you need speed here. The Mites start coming from the bottom soon, too, so it's best to leave the Bubbles alone till they pop by themselves, concentrating only on liberated Mites. The onslaught ends when the Tunnel does. But don't relax: that's when the Bubble Brain attacks. Stay on the left side of the screen, shooting a path through its center to the creature's Brain. Your shots will erode the Bubble; the tiny Bubbles it spews are easily shot. The monster won't charge you if you eat it away relatively quickly.

Watch for the bonus area here. When you enter the Tunnel, keep a lookout for the pit on the bottom, the lower home of the Bubble Mites. Fly down into it and stay to the top: you'll be able to blast pink Bubbles for a slew of golden power-ups. Don't tarry, though: the Pink Bubbles regenerate, and if you're in an area from which they were cleared, you'll perish when they return! You can only get into the pit once during a game.

Zone Three: More waves of ships like the ones you've faced before, then it's into the Lava Them and Leave Them Zone. Shortly after you enter, shoot the Turret on top and watch out for the roving ones that will charge in from the left. When the first one walks onto the scene above, get to its left and shoot it along with the Turrets behind it. When the large Island appears in the middle of the screen, stay to the top of it; projectiles from below will not pass through. Go to the bottom when you reach the next Island, then stay *as much as possible* in the center of the screen so you can shoot everything coming your way . . . and have maneuvering room to avoid the projectiles of ships and Turrets you missed! After the next Island drops down from the top of the Tunnel, get above it—mainly so you don't get crushed beneath the poor man's Laputa—pick off the Turrets, and stay left of center to shoot what's coming at you. Watch out for the orange Pods which shoot projectiles 360 degrees. After the second Island comes from the top, drop down so you can go around the downward-facing Volcano that occupies most of the screen—pick off the Turrets on the bottom first, or you won't make it. Fortunately, you can blast the Lava balls it spits out. Stay level with its maw as you move ahead; once you're past it, shift to the top of the screen, blast the Turrets up there, and pass the upward-facing Volcano next. When you're through here, you're goin' down: diagonally down, to the right. Stay at the very bottom of the screen, shooting the Turrets in front of you; don't worry if you can't shoot the ones behind you—they won't get you.

When the Tunnel straightens, you'll be headed to the right. An Island will come down again: shoot the three Turrets on top and continue right. Shoot your way through the wall of Rock ahead, making adjustments when you can't go anymore. When you're past the section of Rock from which the Island descended, go up ever so slightly and start shooting. Keep shooting as you go through the Rock ahead, blasting the Golden Boulders. You want to come up just under the orange Rock up ahead: it's a Ledge with Turrets, and a Base that throws out ships. (You want to be dead-center with the first Golden Boulder you encounter.) If you're properly lined up, you can pick every enemy off as you move ahead. Don't scroll the Ledge on too quickly: you want to make sure everything's onscreen so you can blast it! There's more Rock beyond—shoot ahead! (Note: throughout this section, if you've got rockets that shoot up, be very careful: they may dislodge Boulders which will crush you!)

When you clear the Ledge and are into the Rock beyond, more ships will attack: don't get trapped in your Tunnel or the projectiles will destroy you. At the end of this ordeal, fly diagonally to the upper right, sniping at the Turrets on the wall ahead, then it's another horizontal passage full of ships. Stay to the top to nail the Bases before they can dispatch ships. Past the first dormant downward-hanging Volcano, get to the middle of the screen and stay there: you'll be circled by Rock Ships, which will orbit you counterclockwise. Pick them off with whatever weapons you have, then hit the Base on the bottom.

Boss time: QB2B comes from the Rock on the right. It fires two Laser Beams and . . . no problem, you think. Just stay between them, firing. Well, QB2B follows them with zigzag Lasers *within* the parallel Beams. They form little diamond shapes—safe areas —and if you're not in one of them, you die. Stay *very* close to the boss—one ship's length should do it—so you'll be in the nearest diamond area.

Hereafter, events come at you too quickly for us to walk you through. Either you can shoot the enemies or you can't! The bosses, however, are a different matter, and here's how to beat them.

Zone Four: This is the Pop Rock Monolith Zone, at the end of which Mega Monolith spits out little (but deadly) Easter Island heads and causes the earth to crumble around you. Since you've got to shoot into the giant's mouth, staying in the middle of the screen serves two purposes: it lets you shoot the maw *and* gives you time to duck anything that's coming at you from different points of the screen. After ducking any given onslaught, get *back* to the middle to ready yourself for the next.

There's also a bonus section in this zone: when you reach the Moai Heads, fly right into the first one on top of the Rock ledge, making sure that none of your power-ups is lit.

Zone Five: The boss of the Light My Fire Zone isn't Jim Morrison: it's the Two-Headed Scorch Serpent. (Maybe it *is* Morrison after all.) Like the Serpentines in Zone One, its head is vulnerable. Unlike the Serpentines in Zone One, it spits tongues of fire. Stay on the left, concentrating on the nearest head and sticking with it. (Staying to the left is something of a rule throughout the zone, especially if your ship is low on defenses: this entire level is like the Volcano region in Zone Three! There are a lot of fireballs coming at you, only this time—like the Bubbles in Zone Two—they bust up into smaller ones. And often in *very* narrow passages between Volcanoes!)

Zone Six: From the Doors to the Beatles (sort of), you'll find yourself not in an octopus's garden, but in Bacterion's Garden. The Hives here are like the Bubbles with Bubble Mites: get them fast or their issue will kill you. The boss is the gross-looking Bulbous. It's a plant with a suction mouth, which means if you go from left to right, crossing the middle of the screen, you're courting destruction. Having said that, the left side, center, isn't the safest place to roost either, since the giant plant can close its jaws around you. Stay in the top left whenever possible, where you only have to dodge its projectiles; when Bulbous's red center is accessible, drop down and blast it.

Zone Seven: The Greased Lightning Round is a trip through your enemy's computer sector. As you move through the narrow passages, dodging projectiles, try to stay in the middle of the screen: you want to have equal access to all areas of the screen to keep from being locked behind closed doors. When you face Beacon, you'll feel like you're back at the end of Zone Three . . . but with a difference. Several, actually. It charges from behind you, heading right: stay in the upper portion of the screen when the battle is nigh. It finally settles in on the right, moving up and down as it fires Lasers *and* Laser Balls at you. *Don't stop moving!* Your primary goal is to avoid being hit; your secondary goal is to get in shots at Beacon's center *when you can!*

Zone Eight: Mayors on Parade: dumb name for a level, but you won't have time to reflect on that. This zone is, in essence, a series of minibosses. The first (unnamed) shoots projectiles that home in on you followed by Lasers; hit it in the "snout" whenever you have a safe shot. The second, Monarch, has two projectile-firing tentacles and a "mouth" that spits Lasers: stay in the center, far left, and when you're not dodging its fire, shoot the creature's center when its tentacles aren't in the way. Next up is Ice Ice, whose rap is truly annoying. This one fires long Laser bullets that range up and down the screen: you've got to stay on the left and do the same, moving constantly to stay out of its way, and getting in your few shots when you can.

After these preliminaries, it's time for the main bout with brother Grim, the boss. Grim fires Ice Ice-like Lasers, and also charges left. Play defense until it goes dormant for a few seconds, on the right. Get in position, ready to zap it when it starts again, then go back on defense. Patience, Nintendoite, is what you need here.

Zone Nine: Stay in the middle left of the screen here, as the landscape tends to narrow suddenly and you'll want to have quick access to safe passage. You'll also face a wall of enemies (literally), and you'll want to be on the far left to give yourself some reaction time. The foes are tough—that's why they call the level The Gauntlet—but they're easy compared to Shadow Dancer. The spidery boss comes from the left: *go* left when it lifts a spindly leg, and stay roughly on the center left. Unfortunately, the creature is called Shadow Dancer because there are two of them, working more or less in tandem. Whatever they throw your way, forcing you to move, get *back* to the left center and keep shooting at their foul blue hearts.

Zone Ten: Bacterion's Lair! The early foes are surprisingly easy, as long as you have some firepower to throw their way. Even more surprising, though, is Bacterion. Like most tyrants, the alien's a pushover: a few shots and the boss of bosses is no more.

A Few Tips: Here are some tips that will let you start the game with some serious advantages. Note: these work with the controllers that come with the Super NES set but *not* necessarily with any outside controllers you might use. However, you *can* program the code on the NES controller, pause the game, then plug another one in. That'll work just fine.

If you want to boost your weapons to the max (naw . . . I don't wanna), press up, up, down, down, then press the top buttons left, right, left, right, holding the right button down. Still holding the button, press and hold B, A, then hit start. You'll be amazed at what your tiny ship can carry! Unfortunately, if you die, you'll lose your weapons and will have to reenter the code to regain them . . . which you can only do once in each level. (Or you can save them up by *not* using this trick in the early zones.)

During the title screen, tap the X button over and over, as fast as you can, then hit start before the screen leaves. You'll be able to boost your credits (continues) considerably. Unfortunately, you can't use this in conjunction with the following title screen maneuver which, ultimately, gives you more ships:

To start with a full thirty ships—that is, 120 ships when you count the continues—go to the title screen: hold the pad to the left, then press the A button three times and hit start. (Actually, you're getting more than thirty lives: each time you hit "continue" after a game, you start out with thirty new ones!)

For some unwanted fireworks, press the pad up, up, down, down, left, right, left, right—holding down right—and, still holding down right, press and hold down B and A. You'll suffer an explosion when you unpause . . . but a *very* colorful one!

If you want your trusty R. Option Shields to cover a wider area, choose the R. Option block and activate it by gathering sufficient power-ups. When it's highlighted, press and hold the A button, and the area covered by the Shield will double right before your eyes!

For those of you who like surprises during the game, go to the weapon screen and hit X, Y, X, Y, X, Y. The game will give you weapons of its own choosing.

For a somewhat *different* game, go to the option screen and hit the A button over and over, as fast as you can. You'll be given the choice of easy, difficult . . . and now arcade! Tackle it, if you're game.

Rating: B

Challenge: A

The game is fast and furious—though there are plenty of opportunities to power-up.

Graphics: C+

Disappointingly ordinary except for a few neat effects (like the Bubbles).

Sound Effects: C+

The sound effects and music both are nothing to write home about—though we could *swear* that's the Rambo theme playing in Zone Two.

Simulation: C+

You'll experience some sensation of flying and firing . . . though the small size of the ship limits the illusion considerably.

HAL'S HOLE-IN-ONE GOLF

Type: Realistic eighteen-hole golf

Objective: Tee off and get the little white ball into the cup!

Heroes: You can select your clubs, adjust your swing, and get a close look at both the contour of the area around the hole—complete with a grid—as well as the hole itself.

Enemies: Your golfing rival, as well as the terrain and wind.

Menu: You can practice or play in various competitive modes which are described in the instructions. The game can even do instant replays!

Scoring: Same as in real golf.

Strategies: It won't take long for you to decide which clubs are best for you. However, there are certain places you should definitely try to land when teeing off:

Hole One: Try to get your ball to the middle of the fairway, slightly below the lowest bunker.

Hole Two: You want to place your ball just to the right of bunker two.

Hole Three: Go for the region beyond the pond and to the left of the bunker on the right.

Hole Four: Pretty straightforward: get over the pond, skewing slightly to the left to make sure you miss the bunker on the right.

Hole Five: It's tough to clear the two bunkers ahead, so you'll have to land in the area between them. If you land a little short, that's still, obviously, better than landing in them!

Hole Six: Aim for the region on top of the middle bunker—the one on the right.

Hole Seven: Try and place the ball to the right of the bunker on the left . . . or slightly beyond it, if possible. You want to be close enough to the pond to get over with your second shot.

Hole Eight: The goal here is straight ahead: go as far as you comfortably can with each shot.

Hole Nine: Be a little conservative here, as you don't want to go sailing over the green into a bunker.

Hole Ten: Shoot so that you clear the pond and land to the lower left of the bunker.

Hole Eleven: Like Hole Eight, fire straight down the fairway.

Hole Twelve: Ideally, you'll want to land in the middle of the three bunkers that girdle the center section of the fairway. Since it will take you at least two strokes to get to the green, it's best to skew to the right, landing short of the bunker there, then clearing it with your second shot.

Hole Thirteen: Reaching the green on your tee-off is unlikely, so go for a shot that will get you just halfway there. Anything more than that—but not quite on the green—will cause your ball to roll into the rough. If you *do* shoot for the green, try to hit it on the left side; if it rolls off the right side, you're in the water.

Hole Fourteen: You've got a lot of water on the left. Tee off toward the right—more than you would on a windless day—just to make sure you aren't blown into the pond.

Hole Fifteen: Hit the ball slightly toward the right, so you'll clear the bunker on the near right but will be sure to land to the right of the higher bunker on the left.

Hole Sixteen: A toughie. There's a bunker on the right, and you want to land clear of it on the left. If you're too far to the right, you'll have trouble clearing the bunkers up by the green.

Hole Seventeen: You don't have any choice here: you've got to land on the green the first time out.

Hole Eighteen: You want to get over the water with your tee shot, and land to the right of the bunker. If you've got to overcompensate to the right, do so: better to land there than on the left with a second, bigger bunker between you and the green.

Rating: A

Challenge: A

The various combinations of wind, terrain, and clubs makes the game different every time you play.

Graphics: A

The play and "analysis" modes are amazing.

Sound Effects: A

Couldn't sound more real if you were out at the club on a sunny day!

Simulation: A

Right down to the sweaty palms, this is as close to the Real McCoy as you can get.

HOME ALONE

Type: Domestic shoot-'em-up

Objective: You're little Kevin, and you've got to race through four levels of the house, each with two floors and a basement, saving all of the household valuables, toys, electronics, and pets before the baddies get them . . . or you.

Heroes: Kevin can run, squat, leap, and fire his Water Pistol—as well as other power-up weapons he finds. Kevin can also use household items such as Banana Peels, Buckets, and Bowling Balls against foes. *Make sure you recapture bullets or Baseballs that bounce off crooks!* They can be reused. Objects such as Beds and Chairs give him an extra boost. He opens drawers to see what's inside by passing back and forth in front of them. Kevin can also collect Pizza, Pizza Boxes, and Cookies, which increase his lives, and After-Shave, which makes him invulnerable for fifteen seconds. All of these items—and the items to be collected—are found in the same place each game. You progress to the next level when every valuable has been collected —according to the screen on the upper right. Kevin's only problem: he can't hold everything, and has to make regular deposits in Laundry Chutes to unburden himself.

Enemies: In addition to Marv, who chases Kevin and steals valuables, and Harry, who only chases Kevin, there are Mobsters who don't chase Kevin but steal or throw things. Note: any criminal you eliminate before you enter a room will be there when you emerge. And a thug about to step in a trap—Tacks, for example—will be spared if you start stuffing things down the Chute before he does so!

Menu: Only one player plays; your only "choice" involves the sound.

Scoring: You earn points for every valuable, toy, etc. you collect, though *not* weapons. (Points are awarded even after you've achieved your "booty requirement," so don't pass anything up.) You also get points for every thug you fell.

Strategies: Regardless of the level or floor, you've got to explore every room—though the order doesn't matter very much. Here are the high points.

Level One: You've got to collect 24 objects here, and the level holds no real surprises. To get the valuable on top of the tall Dresser in the master bedroom, open a drawer and jump from the red chair to the drawer to the Dresser top. And don't leave anything unexplored: there's even Pizza in the Bathtub. When the Ring falls on the Table and you can't get it, just jump up and down beside the table and it will slide toward you. Don't forget to jump up in front of the Painting at the bottom of the steps, leaping against the wall; to look in the Painting to the left of the Toys on the floor; and to check out the Painting over the Chute to the right. Cross the Table in the red room and get the Pizza over the left Chair. After you fulfill your goal—there are more objects than you need, incidentally—there'll be a Key lying on the floor in front of the locked brown door. Enter. Be prepared to duck and leap as Bats and Rats attack you in the basement. In the basement, jockey yourself so that you're never under a Bat: if a Rat comes along, you'll be cornered.

Level Two: The second level has thirty valuables to collect. Here, you're collecting Toys. After finishing in the bedroom, go left to lure Harry over. Run right till he slips over the Tacks, then go left and collect objects; don't forget the Pizza in the pictures over the Train table. In the red room, get a Cookie from the Mirror over the Chest. Watch out in the game room: you're going to be shot at in here! There's After-Shave in the bathroom and Pizza over the Ping-Pong Table. In that same room, run in front of the bookcase on the right, ducking when the thug throws his hat. You can reach the Helicopter by jumping from the very edge of the Ping-Pong Table. When you exit that room, you'll find another Toy in the pictures to the left.

This time the basement's got Spiders. You can jump over the first few, but after that they rise and fall. Jump to make the first Spider drop, then leap over it and, without stopping, run under the second. When you reach the row of three Spiders moving side to side, jump when the Spider on the right is at the right side, then hurry over the next two. At the end, drop Cinderblocks on the giant Spider to destroy it. It'll take five hits to kill the arachnid, and it speeds up after each one, so watch it! (To escape it, hold the controller to the left so that Kevin is hugging the wall. He's safe there.)

Level Three: You've got 35 items to get, and can hold

ten at a time, and now you're going after electronics. Check out the video room thoroughly: there's a Pizza Box in the last set of shelves on the right. There's another in the Toilet of the bathroom. You'll also find After-Shave in the sink. Watch out for the video room on the second floor: the guy with the hat is back, chucking it at you! Get the TV in the upstairs bedroom by jumping on the bed on the right, making a large, arcing leap to the left bed, and leaping from the leftmost edge onto the shelf. You'll find a BB Rifle on the top of a Dresser in the hallway upstairs. Also, look for a slice of Pizza between the two lamps with the Painting of the vase betwixt them.

When you've got the Key, you have to tangle with Ghosts in the basement. Watch the patterns and slip or jump through, just as you did with the Spiders. The big Ghost at the end has to be Cinderblock-clobbered the same as the Spider. You'll be able to win as you did before: running to the left corner and tucking yourself in there when it attacks, rushing back and dislodging the block, running left until it retreats, and so on.

Level Four: Your goal's 35 pets . . . reptiles, amphibians, and little furry critters. And if you killed yourself getting the BB Rifle last level, too bad! There's one in your Dresser in the bedroom. This level introduces Tacks that come in sets of two, side by side, so use the ledges above them, where possible. (You *can* jump between them, but it takes precision leaping.) The thugs also come at you a little faster on this level. There's After-Shave in the bathroom, and you should use it to clear out the place while you're empowered. Otherwise, the thug is a killer and getting to the Bucket to clobber him is tough. On the bottom floor, first door left of the steps, watch out for the hat guy on the left. As for the annoying Bird in the room full of Tables—

second door from the steps, top floor—you *can* get it by leaping off the far edge of the small, rightmost Table.

When you're finished, it's time to tango with more Rats, on the floor and ceiling. Again, watch their patterns and deal with the boss Rat at the end just as you did the other bosses.

Rating: C+

> *Challenge:* C
> Kids will enjoy the first three levels, experienced gamers will get a kick out of the fourth—but once you figure it out, there's no reason to go back.

> *Graphics:* B
> The programmers did a good job with likenesses and animation, and the electronics—complete with flashing numbers—are very good.

> *Sound Effects:* A
> Excellent Tchaikovsky score, and the film's catchphrases are re-created perfectly.

> *Simulation:* C
> There's a very limited sense of reality due to the limited number of moves Kevin can make.

LAGOON

Type: Fantasy quest

Objective: Demons have infested the once-peaceful lands around Atland. Though inexperienced, young Nasir must go forth, visiting different lands and Castles, finding secret items, rescuing kidnap victims, fighting monsters and Demons, and rescuing the Princess Felicia, who has been abducted by the fiend behind the corruption: Zerah.

Heroes: Nasir begins weak and penniless. He gets Gold and buys weapons as he proceeds; he wins other items in combat or by successfully completing missions; and he gains experience—strength and endurance—by killing monsters. When Nasir leads someone around—say Giles, in the Gold Cave, or Thor in Voloh—he can only proceed as fast as they do, which isn't fast. And he can't leave a site unless the person he's leading is nearby.

Enemies: These range from minor monsters that roam the countrysides to stronger ones in the Castles to powerful Demons which run the Castles.

Menu: This is a one-player game. The game can be saved, though.

Scoring: Nasir earns strength in combat, along with power-ups.

Strategies: Begin the game by walking down, below the church, past the fountain, to the Mayor's house, which is to the left; walk past the pool by the bottom wall. Talk to his wife, then head up to the church. Talk to the Mayor, then lend an ear to the newcomer. He'll lead you to a cave and a wounded man. Talk to the prone figure, then talk to the Mayor; return to the town—bottom left of the screen—and go to the church. Tell the Cleric what happened, and return to the Mayor's home. He'll give you 300 Gold: go and buy yourself a Short Sword and Armor in the Armor Shop, behind the church to the upper left. When you've made your purchase, exit the town and enter the Gold Cave ahead. Go left, up, right, up, left, up, left (under the logs), down, left (under more logs), up, left, down. There's a Treasure Chest here: open it for a Healing Pot.

Once you've got that, go up, right, down, right, up, right, up, left, and up into the open door. Go right and down the steps. In the new room go right, past the Skeleton Warrior—one touch from its sword will kill you—and down the first passageway to a new Treasure Chest. Get ten Gold from it. Go back up to the corridor and continue right to the end. Go down, right, up, left, and take the first turn up: enter the door there. Go right and take the steps. You'll find yourself on a series of cliffs: climb the stairs to the top and have a chat with Giles. Give him the Healing Pot and take him home by leading him back through the Gold Cave: into the cliff door, over to the stairs on the left, down through the Skeleton Warrior room, right, down, left, up, left, and up at the door. Once you're through the door, go left, through the door, and right. Head down at the end of the corridor, and continue going down until that hallway ends. Go right, down, left, down, right, and down and out.

As soon as you bring Giles into the town, he becomes a chatterbox. He'll tell you to go see the Faith Healer: she lives in the lower right corner of the town. First, though, stop on the Weapon Shop and buy a Healing Pot to replace the one you lost. Continue down to the Faith Healer and she'll tell you about the demon Samson locked in the cave, and will give you a key with which to let him out. Before going there, head for the Armor Shop and pick up an Iron Shield. Go back for one more talk with the Faith Healer: she'll tell you about a path from Samson to the Elf Field. Still, don't leave Atland just yet: chat with the old woman roaming the streets and learn about the Earth Staff located at the village of Voloh. Then, back into the Gold Cave.

Go left, up, right, up, and left at the second hallway, and up. Use the key, enter, and get a good look at Samson. If you're not up to Level 8, you're not going to be able to do *more* than that! To bring yourself to that level, go around the Cave slaying the monsters you may have missed . . . and, slowly, your meter will fill! (Also look for the twenty Gold Treasure Chest you may've missed in here!) At Level 8, enter the room and strike at the giant red demon's left leg, at the white marking: just get in close and keep sluggin' till he's down. After his death, the door on the other side of the room will open automatically and you'll find yourself in the Elf Field. Make sure there was nothing you needed back in town: an earthquake seals the cave and you can't go back!

Slay the two bugs when you emerge, and brace yourself for more bugs—one crawling breed, the other flying. Get up to Level 9 here, then go through the two campfires straight ahead. You're in Voloh. The first Elf will tell you the location of Philips Castle, and also about the legend surrounding it. He'll tell you about the three Tablets you'll need to break the sleep enchantment that overcomes the Castle: one is in the plain, one near the Castle; and one is held by a man in blue. Other villagers will tell you more: in particular, that the right door has been locked so you can't get to Denegul; that there are demons inside (what else?), and that Princess Felicia has been spirited away! A girl will tell you about a spooky woman who lurks near the Castle.

Head to the Mayor's house at the top of the village —between the two fires. He'll give you an Earth Staff and also a Movable Mantle to give to the people trapped in the Castle. You'll need to purchase the Shiny Ball from the Weapon Shop—if you have enough Gold. After doing these things, head to the left and locate Thor—not the Norse god, but a young blond lad. In blue. With a piece of Tablet. He'll give you the Tablet of Faith and agree to accompany you. Return to the Elf Field and, while you fight bugs, let Thor find the Tablet of Wish. Head to the right: you'll find that the Elf Field has opened up considerably since last you were here! While you're here, fight your way up to Level 11: use the trees strategically to get to the vulnerable sides of your insect foes. When you're at Level 11, head to the right in the field, then up. With Thor by your side, leave the top of the screen: you'll be in Philips Castle.

Be ready to jump here: not all of the stairs are whole—which means Thor won't be going inside with you. . . . Before you reach the Castle proper, go left and leap the bridgeless chasm: there's a Treasure Chest on the other side. In it is the Tablet of Hope. Tell Thor about it, then take it back to the village and the old Elf there. He'll tell you the magic spell that will let you into the Castle, and bold Thor will leave. Return to the Field, bring yourself up to Level 12, and go to the Castle. Utter the spell and enter. *Draw* a map as you make your way through here, since you're going to have to retrace your steps at one point.

You'll notice Statues as soon as you enter: these are scattered throughout the Castle and should be used as a respite against enemy attacks. Simply get behind them when you need to regain your energy . . . or want to hide from fireball attacks! Knights will attack you in here, but are easily dispatched. Go left, up the door, right, up the door, up the door, up the door, up the long corridor, and right at the end. New kind of Knight to the right: big and powerful. Continue right and go down at the door. Enter the room, slay the big Knight, and open the Treasure Chest. You'll be rewarded with Gold Armor. Go up, left, down. Go down through the door, all the way to the right, and up the door. Go left and up the door. Another Treasure Chest, this one with the Key of Prison. Go down, right, down through the door, and left. Continue past the wide corridor on the bottom and go down the first door beyond it. Go down again, then left and down through the door. Head right, past the front door, and up the first door. Keep going up, through several rooms, until you can't go any further, then go right, up, left. Go down to another Treasure Chest: this one's got 200 Gold. Go right, down, left, and back down to the main corridor. Go right and up the next door. Enter the door at the top of the room and you'll find yourself in a new section of the Castle.

There are new foes here: squidlike wraiths. Go down to the end of the corridor and left. At the very end of the corridor follow the wall up and enter the hallway on top. Go up and right; be prepared to face your first fireball-throwing Wizard. Keep going up. At the top of this corridor, go left and up. Follow the corridor up—it sweeps to the upper left diagonally—and go right at the end. Go up at the end and left . . . quite a long way. Go down the corridor at the end and keep going down. At the end, make your way right to another Chest. (It's to the right of an area with rows of fat columns.) You'll get another 200 Gold. Go left and up at the end of the corridor: you'll find the Jail here. Use the Keys, enter, and talk to the three prisoners. Use the Movable Mantle on the middle one, accept the Key of Philips—which opens the door which leads to the Castle's second floor—then head for the door in the first part of the Castle. Go down, right, up after the Columns, right, up, left, up, right, and up: open another Treasure Chest here for 100 Gold. Go down, right, down, left, and at the end of the corridor go up. Here you can go up or right: go up, right, up. Take the long corridor right and keep going right, through the Wizard area, till you can't go right anymore. There's a wraith and a Treasure Chest: you'll get 130 Gold here. Go down, left, up. Go left, down, right, down, right, and immediately go down. Go left and right down, all the way to the end, then right and up. You're back at the door now . . . and should be at or near Level 14.

Go down, left to the end of the corridor, and up at the Statues. Go left, up through the door at the end, right, up, right, and there's the door to the second floor. Use the Key of Philips to enter. Watch it up here: there are no walls in some places, and if you charge ahead, you could fall to your death! Go down, kill the floating ghoul—a new breed of monster guardian for you!—and keep going down. At the end of the corridor go left, down at the end—staying on the right side of the floor, since the left side ends—then go right (facing a new foe, an electrical "brain"). Go down, then down to the left of the large chamber.

Go left, down, and right. At the end of the corridor go up . . . and keep going up to the end. There's a Treasure Chest with 100 Gold. Go down, left, down at the end, and left: there's a door up ahead. It belongs to the boss, Natela, only you don't want to go in there unless you've hit Level 14. So work on that, then come back here. When you fight the twoheaded monster, attack the gold head only: charge it, then back up with it, hacking away at its snout. When you've defeated the creature, you'll be rewarded with a Silver Sword. Return to the first floor and exit, slashing your way to Level 15 as you go. Exit the Castle, but don't go back to the village. Go right and enter the open door there. Step on the symbol in the floor and you'll be whisked to another room. Enter the door at the top and you'll find yourself in—

The Dwarf Desert. The foes here are tough: not only are there stony plants, they set up electrical barriers right before they spit fireballs. And there are wolves to boot—meant *both* ways. Take your time going through here or the fleet canines will cut you down. Go left and up, using the crannies in the rocks to regain your strength if you get hit hard. (These are also a good place from which to attack the wolves, since you're protected on three sides. Or back *them* in there if you can.) Go left and zigzag through the desert, toward the top to Denegul. (If you see the wall and can't get in, go down and around the outcroppings until you can. The entrance will be on the top.)

There, talk to people: an elder will tell you about the Moon Blade, which you'll need soon, and he'll give you an Ancient Book. He'll also tell you about the Moon Stone located in the Dwarf Cave and give you the Sky Staff. Go to the Armor Shop and buy the Sonic Armor and the Great Shield, and then go and have a talk with your old friend Thor. He'll tell you about his lost Pendant, and you'll offer to go back to

Voloh to find it. There, talk to the Elf wandering to the upper right of the elder Elf: you'll get the Pendant. When you bring it back to butterfingers—taking time to boost yourself to Level 16 en route—he'll give you a powerful Mirror. Since it can smash rocks, you'll be able to enter the Cave, which is to the right—return to the entrance to the Desert, then go up and right. As you make your way to the Cave, build yourself to Level 17.

At the Dwarf Cave, L-button away the Rocks using the Mirror and enter. Watch your step: like the Castle, the floors aren't exactly safe. There are holes all over through which you can see boiling Lava below. Cross the first cavern, leaping ahead where necessary, until the end. You'll be spirited to another cavern. You'll have to cross to the end of this one too, sometimes leaping left to right; your goal is in the top left. Land on the platform there and you'll be transported to another cavern. With monsters. Some walk the land and shoot Lava balls—don't get in front of them and you'll be okay—others fly up from the seething rock, grab you in their jaws, and drag you into the Lava; if you hit them as you're pulled along, they'll die—or, better yet, just walk through with your sword swinging! Though you can walk out of the Lava—except if you fall off a cliff—it will cost a lot of energy. Keep going ahead till you get to an isthmus headed right: cross it and jump to an island with a Treasure Chest. It will give you a Magic Sword. Continue right, then go up and enter the inner Cave. Wait till your power's fully charged, then follow the *walk* to the left. Stay on it, leaping where necessary, until you reach another Treasure Chest: inside is a Wind Crystal. But don't leave yet: cross to the upper right side of the chamber to the Treasure Chest with the Protective Ring, get it, then follow the path down and around to the right, then up. Hack away until you're at Level 18, continuing around to the right, then down, then into the Cave mouth.

You're now in the Silence Cave. Go to the far side and get the Moon Stone from the wall. Exit the Cave the way you came. When you're on the narrow strip of land in the next section, go down and then to the right: it will bring you to a plate that will send you back to the Desert. Return to Denegul and talk to Mathias, just inside the door; he'll tell you that Felicia is in the Dwarf Cave, having been taken there by a woman named Ella who works for Zerah. Then go show the old man (from before) the Moon Stone. He'll give you a Freezing Pot in return for letting him see it: this will open the part of the Dwarf Cave blocked by Lava. So—

Back to the Cave. Build yourself up to Level 19 as you go, then enter and return to where you got the Wind Crystal. To the lower left is an area of surging Lava; stand on the land below it, hit the L button with the Freezing Pot, and a road will appear, allowing you to enter a new Cave. Talk to Felicia. She'll tell you about the plot to move Lagoon Castle and use its hidden magic to destroy the world; unfortunately, before you can take her out of here, Ella comes along and sneaks her away. Follow them: all roads lead to the boss here, Eardon. Fight the monster—having first switched to your Moon Stone and built yourself to Level 20—by hacking its beam-shooting eyes when they emerge.

After killing the creature, you'll be admitted to Hobbit Valley—did they get the rights to *use* this name? Fuzzy Eyeballs and Axe-throwing Boar people await. Head up through the valley to Poper. You'll find the town disease-ridden and will learn that to cure the people, you'll have to get some Mint from Siegfried Castle . . . which, needless to say, is guarded by demons. Leave the city and go down, then to the upper left of Hobbit Valley. You'll pass to a new section of the valley: head left and up and you're at the Castle.

The Knights move faster in here than you're used to, and there are bowling ball things that roll at you. Enter, go all the way to the right and all the way up. There's a door above and one below: the one above leads you to a new section. For now, take the one below. Go left and down to a Treasure Chest with a Defensive Ring. Leave and go left, down past the first corridor, turn right into the second, and go up into the first room: the Treasure Chest will give you a Force Sword. Go back to the door that leads to the new section and enter when you're at Level 21. The Batlike guards in here are burly but easier than the multiarmed guards, whose swords will cut you up in a hurry. Go left, down, into the room, and right: there's a Treasure Chest with Thunder Armor. Once you've got that, get the Mint by returning to where you entered this section and going straight down on the right. You'll soon reach the room with the Treasure Chest—you'll see a familiar empty Chest on your way. . . . Return to the village with your Mint. Enter the Worship Site, give the Mint to the Cleric, and he'll tell you to enter one of the Stained Glass Windows. Do so, and you'll talk with several people, one of whom will give you the Star Staff. Another will inform you that Siegfried Castle is controlled by the Demon Duma. You'll be told to go to the third floor of the Castle, find the Warp, and go upstream. However, to get through the locked second floor, you'll need a key—which, happily, this good soul gives to you.

Back at the Castle, you don't have to go far: go to the right side of the corridor, up and left—*not* to the door that leads to the second section—and left to the wall with the symbols on a silvery door-sized panel. That's the room! Raise yourself to Level 25—while you're doing that, go back and search the section with the bat guards: there's another Treasure Chest in a room right below the door where you enter, and it's got a Power Ring. Then use the Key to enter and fight Duma: run up when the giant head appears, get in your licks when the faceplate is open, then back away when the giant's hands try to clap you between them; duck the fireballs by cutting slightly to the right after they're fired—your move is a big L shape. Move in when the hands retreat and repeat until Duma is dead. It's a good idea to use the Moon Stone here: you'll defeat the beast in four blows! You'll be rewarded with the Water Crystal and Key of Siegfried; use the latter down the hall to the left and up. Climb the stairs, and when it doesn't seem as though you can go anywhere, go down into the wall. You'll reappear in another section of the Castle. The guards here are *big* warriors and Robots who fire deadly Laser Beams; don't take any of them lightly! Travel straight down and right at the bottom. Go up the corridor at the very end and it leads to an entranceway. Go in and find out some distressing news about Thor . . . and the Castle. Fortunately, the Warp plate is also here, and it will take you to the Gnome Tree. Go straight ahead and enter the Tree, which brings you to Lilaty.

The people will tell you about the Ice Cave, about the Nymphs . . . and will give you an Angel's Bell to call them after you defeat the Demons in the Ice Cave. Make sure you go to the upper right part of the village, get the Truth Fire, and use it on the liar you encounter. Answer "No" when he asks his question— He'll give you the Fur Mantle you'll need for the Ice Cave.

Cross the Gnome Plain and enter the Cave—with your Fur Mantle on. There are wicked Gnomes in here: they're tough too. So are the Roses in a Vase: the

Vases turn to jelly and chase you with the fireball-spitting Roses still inside. Go up on the left and enter the door. Once inside, don't walk into the pits of water or you'll drown. Go right, up, right, up, right, down, right, and up for a Treasure Chest with 250 Gold. Leave and go left, up, left, and up until you reach a point with a Rose in the room above and one to the left. Go left. Head slightly down and continue left, then go up. Turn left where the Gnome is waiting and go up until you reach the boss's door. Don't go in yet: there are two things you have to do. First, make sure you're at Level 30. Second, while you're doing that—it's going to take a considerable amount of time—make for the right side of the Cave and find the Treasure Chest with the Bright Stone. (Get there by finding the room with the three frozen Flames and then going up, left, up, right, down.) When you've got it and are back at the boss's room, enter and watch the patterns of the Ice bullets being fired at you and hack at each of the six globes between shots . . . crossing to them when the giant snowball isn't rolling. Start by getting off the path and going to the lower right, to the left, just below the Dome there. Watch the pattern and destroy the dome from the front when you can, after standing to its side to draw its fire in that direction. When that's done, make your way to the left and get the Dome there, then go up and get the center right Dome. Next tackle the one on the left. Go around it to the left and get the one on the top left, then right. Use the "safe zones" as you make your way up: the outcroppings of Ice to the far left or right where the Ice can't hit you. When you're finished with the six domes, the "snowball" will become the monster Thimale—actually, a transparent ball with a giant eye spitting Ice. Get to the bottom—using the Elixir, if you have to—stand in front of the beast and hit it four times to destroy it. You'll get the Life Ball and can exit to the Nymph Spring. Go to the top of the island and use the Angel Bell there: the Nymphs will arrive to tell you where Zerah is headed and give you the Moon Staff. They'll also whisk you to Phantom Hill.

As you climb, you'll fight deadly birds and dead ends. Go up, right, up, up, up on the right, up on the right, up on the left, up on the left, up, and you'll reach a hole. Enter an old "friend" who won't let you go any further. Ella will throw fireballs at you and vanish and reappear elsewhere—but on the whole, she's easy to destroy, especially if you've gotten yourself up to Level 32. Exit the chamber on the bottom and a Ladder will appear to allow you to continue up Phantom Hill. Jump to the right cliff and you'll find Zerah. Fortunately, you won't have to fight the powerful wizard: Mathias will arrive and the two will knock each other out. Zerah will escape, but Mathias will tell you your life story, give you the Thunder Crystal, and send you off to the Cloud.

You've got to leap from Cloud to Cloud up here. Make your way up and, at the Waterfall, jump down to the green island. That's where Lagoon Castle is located. Go up to the platform and you'll learn that when the moonlight enters the Castle's terrace, you must hold the Moon Stone to acquire the Moon Blade. Enter the Castle ahead. There are reptile-people for guards, along with floating slugs, Jesters, and other nasties. Go to the door at the top left of this level. *Don't* enter yet: go down the corridor to its left and exit left. There's another section with a door on the upper left. Enter it, go to the left, and enter the Silence Terrace. Go over to the beam of light, take out the Moon Stone, and you'll get the Moon Blade. There's an exit to the right, but you won't be going here yet. Return to the other door and enter that. There are big, new guards in here; whack away until you're up to

Level 35, then look around in the center for the room with the King of the Castle. (It's a big room with a black top: when you find it, you'll know.) He'll tell you that Felicia is trapped in a mirror on the fourth floor, and that the only way to save her is to find the Statue that must be used on the Crest in the room where Felicia is trapped: he'll emphasize that you must use it while facing her. Search for it while building yourself up to the final level, Level 35; you'll find the Statue in a Treasure Chest in an area down and right from the King's chambers. Once you've got it, go back to the Silence Terrace and exit to the right. Go straight, up, down at the second downward passageway, and down to the first hallway on the left. Enter for a Treasure Chest with 350 Gold—why not? Return to the main hallway on the right and continue down. At the next corridor to the left, enter, go up, left, down, left, down, right, and you'll find a doorway. Enter. Get Elixir from the Treasure Chest at the bottom, then go up.

You'll face the strongest monsters yet in here: big green guards and spidery green cyclopes. To get to the Mirror, go up, right, down, and right . . . all the way to the end. Go up to the end, left to the end, down, left, down, right, and up into the arch. L-button the Statue to save Felicia, then talk to her. She'll tell you about Zerah and Thor, and will tell you to walk through the Mirror. Do so. Madness reigns inside: the Knights are tremendous, but at least they're slow. To find Zerah, go down, right, down, left, and down. Take the door and go down, right, and up into the door. Battler's there, with two huge aides. Avoid the big eyes by hiding in the door nook to the rear; when you can, hit Zerah in the sides. (You'll want your Life Stone handy when you challenge the boss.) The two mono-orbed flunkies will die when Battler does. Enter the door on top, leap to the little green patch ahead, then continue up. Talk to the old man in the building, then head to the stairs on the left.

Follow the cavern, past the most powerful fiends—despite being at Level 35, you'll die in an instant. Go left, down—you might pass the narrow land if you hurry—and left, following the ledge around the cliff. Pause to recharge along the way so your strength meter is always full. Continue left and make your way up: you'll get a Time Ring from the next Treasure Chest. Then head back to the right and make your way down: you're looking for a long passageway that leads to the left. At the end, go up. You're taking yourself to an area where two guards—who look suspiciously like Marvel Comics' Thor—stand by a golden door. Enter and, leaping the first flurry of fireballs, hit the fiend in its shiny red nose. It'll lose no energy but will flash; when you've gotten in your blows, it'll change to a winged demon that tries to whip you with its tail. Get behind it and hit its back—sorry, honorable warrior, but that's how it's done. If you've got Elixir, you'll win with no problem. When it dies, the wall will open behind it and you'll face Thor and Zerah. Kill him in his monster form with six or seven blows, then fight Thor. When you've beaten him—leaping the flames and moving in between the bullets—he'll turn into a huge white bird firing blasts at you: you've got to lick this creature too before peace can be restored to the kingdom.

Rating: A–
> *Challenge:* A
>> Wonderful for beginning role-players; experienced players will have fun discovering all its secrets.
>
> *Graphics:* A
>> The view is from overhead, and the cartoon animation is superb, the settings very evocative.

Definitely *not* for videogamers with vertigo, however!

Sound Effects: C–

Nothing to cause much excitement; the 1960s spy music is blah, and the "ping" of the sword is uninspired.

Simulation: A–

You'll *definitely* feel like you've been through this world, though the sword swinging feels a little rinky-dink.

THE LEGEND OF ZELDA: A LINK TO THE PAST

Type: Fantasy quest

Objective: After all that the land of Hyrule has been through, you'd think they'd get a break. Uh-uh. The sorcerer Agahnim has conquered the realm and made off with several damsels—including Princess Zelda. Not content with dominating Hyrule, however, Agahnim is attempting to create a doorway between the kingdom and the Dark World. If he succeeds, his powers will be enormous! Naturally, there's only one person who can stop him. Contacted telepathically by Zelda, Link heads out to save the world once again.

Hero: Link is the same spunky hero he's always been, but he has some new abilities and variations on old ones this time around. Among the more important items in his arsenal are the Whirling Blade maneuver, which cuts in a wide arc; Bombs; the Ice Rod, enabling you to turn enemies into fudgsicles; Pegasus Shoes, which grant you super speed; a Hook Shot for swinging across pits, gathering objects just out of your reach, or clobbering distant foes; and the inspired Bug Net, which lets you capture Insects which you can store and unleash on enemies. The most important artifacts you'll be collecting are the Pendants: when you've acquired them all, head to the Lost Woods, where you'll be able to get the all-important, all-powerful Master Sword.

Enemies: There are a lot of them, from unliving foes like rock slides to monsters like Sand Worms, Zombies, and the Armos Kings, which are large warriors. You'll meet them all soon enough.

Menu: There's only the one-player game.

Scoring: Link builds his life meter, stash of Rupees, and skills as he fights his way through the game.

Strategies: Newcomers to the Link mythos will have a tough time with this: even a book the size of the OED wouldn't tell you quite all you need to know! For seasoned gamers, here are the fundamentals to get you going at various levels.

In addition to picking up bushes, Bombing walls (look for telltale fissures), and moving objects like Headstones on graves (and being ready to fight the enemies that *might* lurk beneath them), winning *The Legend of Zelda: A Link to the Past* depends upon knowing your way around Hyrule and being able to find who or what you need.

Hyrule is divided into the Light World and the Dark World.

You begin in the Light World, which is laid out as follows. Note that the order they're discussed below is just *one* way to explore them. As you get used to the game, you'll find variations which may serve you better.

When you start, you're in Link's House. There are several routes you can take: some players will prefer to go right to the Hyrule Castle. If so, refer to that section. Others will prefer to go to the Lost Woods. In any case, start by getting the Lantern in the house. If you choose to start in the Lost Woods—

While you travel through them, make sure you use Dash against the Trees, in order to earn bonuses and power-ups from them. Apart from these, the Woods offer you a great deal. In the south find the Fortune Teller. Follow the road below it to the east and you'll reach the Whirlpool, the location of the Water Warp which will let you warp to Lake Hylia. North of this is the Tunnel which leads to Death Mountain—more on which later. North of that you'll come to the hut of the Lumberjacks, and they're okay! Talk to them about the tree they're cutting down, which is southwest of the hut.

Also in the Woods: move through the Mists to the Den of Thieves, where you'll find an item which is important to your quest. Most important, however, is the Master Sword, which is located in the northern section of the Woods. You'll need it—but you won't be able to get it without the three Pendants.

Go south from the Fortune Teller's hut and you'll come to Kakariko Village. At the top of the village, in the west, is the Thieves' Den; to the east is the home of Sahasrahla. The Thieves' Den is important: don't leave without searching the walls (on top), then use a Bomb to get to a treasure behind the door.

Moving south through the village, you'll find the Weather Vane below the Thieves' Den, the Bottle Merchant to the west, and a House to the west of that. To the east of the Vane is another House. Below the Vane to the West is a House; below it to the east is the Sick Boy's House. (Make sure you search the Houses: if you enter the house on the east side of the village square and tug the picture on the wall on top, you'll get twenty Rupees!)

Get a Bottle from the merchant, then go to the Sick

Boy and talk to the bedridden child. He'll lend you his Bug Net, which you can use to fill your bottle.

Below the Sick Boy's House is the Inn, which is important: if you enter through the lower, main entrance, you can talk to the people inside. However, you must use the information they give you to find another entrance which leads to the storeroom. There, you'll find a Chest with an important item.

Go west from here, and you'll pass an Item Shop and reach a Mysterious Hut. It *seems* to have no entrance, but you can get in by using a Bomb to blow a hole in the wall. Or how about Dashing through weak walls?

To the far east of the Inn, past the water, is the Smith. Alone, the fellow can't help you. But if you check back now and then you'll find that his coworker can put a nice strong edge on your blade!

Directly under the Inn, on the other side of the trees, you'll find the House of Books. Don't leave without retrieving the Book of Mudora which is lying by itself on top of the bookcase. Below the House of Books to the west is the House of the Brothers. The two of them are sulking in separate rooms: blast the wall between them, patch up their differences, and you'll be rewarded. To the east of this hut you'll find the Game of Chance.

Don't leave the village without having obtained two Bottles.

To the east of the village, nestled within the trees, is the Haunted Grove. You can't do much here—i.e., deal with the woodland creatures or the flutist—until you've gone to the Dark World and returned here.

If you continue to the east, you'll come to a familiar place: Link's House. North of this is Hyrule Castle, which is where you should begin your quest (and, later, return to defeat Agahnim). Here's what you must do when you first go there. Chat with the soldiers around the castle, and with their help—along with what Zelda already told you, telepathically, about a secret passageway—go searching for it. You might (hint! hint!) want to try the east side of the castle, top.

Inside, make your way around the bottom level and rescue Zelda from her cell (after first defeating the guard, using the trusty Boomerang you acquire or tossing handy objects at him: this is one dude you *don't* want to get in close to). Once you've freed Zelda, do *everything* she tells you in order to escape the castle. (Later, when you return to kill the fiendish Agahnim, you must use the wizard's own powerful spell against him!) Don't leave here without also having gotten the Sword, Shield, and Magic Cape.

When you've made your way out and explored the Graveyard to the north (moving Headstones to reveal objects . . . and also enemies) your destination will be—

the Desert of Mystery, which is located below Kakariko Village (diagonally south and west from Link's House). There are Vultures and Sandmen here, but you shouldn't have much trouble with them.

In the far northwest of the Desert you'll find the Desert Palace. Your problems here can be summed up in two words: the Locks. To open the main doorway, you'll need to use the Book of Mudora. Inside the palace, you'll be able to get past the lock near the end and face the master of the Palace by using your Lantern to light the Torches. To beat the Lanmolas (sand worms), use your Bow and Arrow: these take longer to work than the Sword, but they let you keep your distance. Spin is also useful.

Don't leave the Palace until you've obtained the second Pendant.

To the east of the Desert Palace is the Desert Cave, and to the lower east of that is the Faeries' Spring.

You'll want to visit the Spring as soon as possible: if you capture a Faerie and put her in a Bottle, you'll have the power to revive Link if he dies. To the east of the Spring is the Sleeping Man. Tug on his post to get his attention. (Later on, you'll want to come back and take the sign.)

To the east of the Desert of Mystery—and directly below Link's house—is a Swamp (to the southeast of the Haunted Grove). There, you'll find the Whirlpool that hides Water Warp, which will let you go directly to the Magic Shop. Below that are the Ruins, which you'll definitely want to explore: inside, you'll find out how to drain the water from the swamp. (If you find any stranded fish, get them back into the water for a bonus!) As you travel through this region, look for sections of the rock walls you can blast for power-ups. Don't leave here without obtaining the Lamp and Flute.

Now, if you go north from Hyrule Castle you'll come to Death Mountain, home of the third Pendant. At its base, to the west, is the Sanctuary; to the east of that, by the *second* Cave over, is the Whirlpool which will take you to Lake Hylia. Above the Sanctuary, to the west—on the ground, not on the Mountain—is the Death Mountain entrance. Inside this long Tunnel, you'll encounter an Old Man who will give you an important item.

In the northwest corner of the Mountain is a passageway to Kakariko Village. Use this if you have to stock up on anything back there. Below it, to the east, is the entrance to the Mountain Cave; above it, to the top, are the Spectacle Rocks. Above that, to the east, is the Tower of Hera. (To get in, you may want to use the Magic Transporter and the Magic Mirror. But you *must* get inside: the third Pendant is in here!) Inside, you'll have to drop through holes in the floor to reach some levels; be sure to go plunge into the Faeries' Spring in the cellar.

The other keys to getting through the Tower are using your Boomerang to eliminate barriers (by hitting the switches), collecting the Moon Pearl, and beating Moldorm by destroying its tail with blow after blow from your Sword.

Make sure you cross to the other side of the Mountain and explore there as well. (You'll have to obtain the Hookshot in order to cross the broken Bridge.) You don't want to leave the Mountain without having added Ether and the Magic Mirror to your arsenal!

Below the Tower is the Portal which leads to the Dark World. Is it time to go there yet? Why not! Have a look around, then use the Mirror to come back if need be.

To the east of Hyrule Castle, past the River, you'll find several important sites in the north. Follow the River as it runs to the east and you'll come to a Magic Shop. Magic and Life Potion are available here. Where the River turns north, you'll find a Whirlpool and the Water Warp which will scoot you to Lake Hylia (it's located directly north of the narrow channel, due west of the *bottom* of the green section of land to the east); to the northwest of that is the Waterfall of Wishing, where the Faerie has the power to transmute certain objects into more useful objects. Zora's Falls are to the east of the Waterfall of Wishing, though it'll cost you plenty—five hundred Rupees—for what you can get (and will *need* to get) there.

Due east of the Hyrule Castle is the Eastern Palace. The entrance to it is in the northeast corner; before you go in, visit the northwest where you'll find Sahasrahla's hiding place and make your way through every square inch of the maze-like cliffs surrounding the entrance: there are important things to find here. Look in the room just to the west of the Palace for the Key you'll need, though be advised that you can't kill the enemies hovering close to the Key. Also, make sure you earn the Long Bow before you face the more powerful creatures inside.

The last important region of the map of Hyrule's Light World are Lake Hylia and environs. You'll need to get the Icerod and a Bottle here. On the shore to the west (technically, still in the swamp) are the Fortune Teller's hut (you'll have to pay for information, which isn't really worth it) and above it, to the northeast (between the Lake and the River) is the Shop. On the Island in the middle of the Lake, you'll find the Fountain of Happiness: come loaded with Rupees and keep pitchin' them into the water until you get what you need. Below that is the Whirlpool with the Water Warp that will take you to the Waterfall of Wishing; the Whirlpool with the Water Warp that'll get you to the Lost Woods is due east of that, to the east of the peninsula. Directly north of that Water Warp Whirlpool is the Ice Cave; to the north and northwest of that are a pair of Faeries' Springs.

Now that you've covered all of the Light World, you'll have to face the Dark World. The deal here is this: Agahnim has trapped seven wise men and locked them inside Crystals. They've got to be freed.

The first Crystal is inside the Dark Palace. After you make your way through the Maze, get the Hammer inside; without it, you'll get nowhere. Have an ample supply of Bombs as well, and move or blast anything that doesn't look solid in order to collect what's behind or below it.

The boss of this Palace is the Helmasaur; it dwells in the first of the two Basements and can be defeated only if you first destroy its Mask using Bombs. After that, your sword and Spin will slay the beast.

If you've gone this far, you'll be able to go the distance using the skills and weapons you've acquired, and remembering two basic rules: talk to people, and blow things up!

Rating: A

Challenge: A

You'll spend a *long* time on this one, and enjoy every exciting minute of it!

Graphics: B+

The graphics add sophistication to the look of the original games without destroying their charm. Still a *bit* too skimpy on details here and there, but that's a minor complaint.

Sound Effects: B

If you liked what the earlier games had (and we did!), here's more of the same.

Simulation: B—

The Link adventures don't try to "put you in the game" as much as others, though there are times when you *will* feel like you're in the hero's shoes.

PILOTWINGS

Type: Aerial hijinks

Objective: Whether you're piloting a Light Plane, using a Hang Glider, Parachute, Rocket Belt, or Helicopter, you have to pass through or clear various hurdles and make precision landings.

Heroes: Your character has complete control of the speed, braking, pitch and yaw, and direction of whatever form of flight is being used. You must "certify" on each level before you can pass to the next.

Enemies: Wind, targets, ineptitude.

Menu: There is only the one-player game, though you can retry failed efforts.

Scoring: You earn points for accuracy, time, and goals accomplished.

Strategies: You'll get the feel of the controls very quickly, and will see right off the bat what has to be done.

In case you have trouble getting to the various levels, however, here are the passwords you'll need:

Level Two: 985206
Level Three: 394391
Level Four: 520771
Helicopter Mission: 108048

These are the codes in the expert mode:

Level Six: 400718
Level Seven: 773224
Level Eight: 165411
Level Nine: 760357
Helicopter Mission: 882943

There are bonus stages in this game, which are as follows:

When parachuting, land on the platform beside the bull's-eye: not only will you earn 100 points, you'll be spirited to a bonus area where you've got to help a Penguin dive into a pool. Fail, and you'll leave a Penguin-shaped hole in the concrete—it's almost worth blowing it to see that.

During the Rocket Belt phase of the game, finish everything successfully and land back on the platform where you began. You'll earn 100 points as well as go to a special Trampoline stage.

Complete the hang-gliding game, land on the platform, and you'll go to a special flying area.

Other nifty tricks:

If you set down on the white domes while using the Rocketbelt, you won't lose any points and can still vault back into the sky.

In the Helicopter phases of play, fly very low to avoid the guns.

Rating: A
  Challenge: A
    Will keep you on your toes every time you play.
  Graphics: A
    Couldn't be better from landscapes to animation.

Sound Effects: A
   Hip score, incredible wind and engine sounds!
Simulation: A
   You'll feel everything but the wind in this game.
   Not for the fainthearted!

SUPER CASTLEVANIA IV

Type: Monster shoot-'em-up

Objective: Every hundred years, the evil vampire Dracula comes back from the dead to terrorize Transylvania—hmmmm . . . seems like every *few* years to us! Only the Belmont family has the daring to tackle the vampire, so once again it's Simon Belmont into the breach. . . .

Heroes: Simon starts the game with a Whip and the ability to walk, jump, crouch . . . and *moonwalk*! (Move him backwards, up the stairs.) Along the way, he picks up other weapons as well as food to keep him going. In any given level, Simon can recross any terrain he's already covered, meaning he can go back for items he's left behind. If Simon dies, he loses all the Hearts he's collected to that point. Also, while the Watch stops most enemies, it *doesn't* render them harmless. If you run into one, it'll hurt you just as if they hadn't been frozen. Among the weapons, Boomerang is best if you're racing against the clock: you get hits going and returning. *Finally, this isn't explicit in the instructions, so take note:* you can lengthen or shorten the Whip while swinging on Hooks. Do this by pressing up (shorten) or down on the controller. Build up speed by pressing the pad left and right. That'll save you a lot of near-misses!

Enemies: Ghouls galore, some requiring just one Whip, others requiring more. Many of these are pictured in the instruction booklet . . . though you'll meet most of them soon enough. Three words of caution: fireballs breathed by monsters can go through stone; Bones flung by Skeletal Knights will survive their death; and when you backtrack, monsters you killed usually reappear!

Menu: There's only a one-Simon game.

Scoring: Simon gets points for every monster defeated. He races against a timer, and Simon will lose a life if it runs out.

Strategies: Here's the adventure, level by level:

Stage One: Get the Sword on top of the stairs, and watch out for the crumbling bridge beyond. Inside the Castle, use the doors in the gate to avoid the bottomless pits you'll encounter on the near side. Use the doors ahead to get back to the foreground—pressing on them as if you were entering, not exiting. Make sure you look in the Vines as well, since there are important items hidden there—such as a Cross, which can be found after you jump down the three ledges near the end, above the left side of the third and lowest ledge. After killing the first Skeletal Knight inside the Castle, go under the steps, whip the Blocks, and get a Small Pork Chop—and an Axe in the Candle before it. Whip up to kill the Knight above you, then go left and up. Go upstairs at the end, take a practice swing on the Hook overhead, and continue to the right. Get close to the green monster, to cause it to emerge from behind the Block, then kill it. Swing across the first Bottomless Pit, get Roast Beef when you land on the column, swing across the second Pit, and duck on the other side to kill the fire-breathing Dragonhead. Descend at the end: break the wall at the very bottom of the stairs—to the left of the Knights— for the Double-shot. Destroy the Dragonhead at the end and exit.

The second Candle has a Firebomb. When you enter the Stable, watch out for the three falling Viper Swarms beyond (a set of two, then one): even if they miss you, they come crawling after you. (You can whip them while they're still aloft, if you're game.) It's a good idea to get to the right of them both, then turn, whip them both, and go back for the Candles. The first Mr. Heds appear after the third Viper Swarm, slithering along the ground. Watch for the first one and kill it before it stirs from under the stones above you—right after the columns. There are three on the ground and one hanging over you. Break the wall at the end for a Big Heart. Upstairs, Medusa Heads come flying at you from the right. As you hit them and go right—or duck them when they're high, jump them when they're low—watch out for the Trapdoors ahead: if you land on one, it'll spill you to your death. Since the Heads will butt you back, don't stand near the Trapdoors when they come floating along. Make sure you get the Candle right before the fifth Window: there's a Small Pork Chop inside. Watch out for the two creatures that come flying at you one at a time after the Trapdoors—stand back until they form, then whip away; they take two hits to kill—and don't fall down the Trapdoor after you leap off the logs at the end. Beware the last Viper Swarm on your way down. Downstairs, beware the Viper Swarm that awaits you right after the Trapdoor: kill it while you're above it by whipping down. Get past the Trapdoors here and it's time to face the boss.

To begin with, crouch on the ledge on the left and kill the Horse—whipping its fireballs to destroy them. The skeletal rider, Rowdain, will dismount: hit at him, but get out from under him when he jumps. He'll pretend to die when he has just a hint of life left: don't fall for it!

To get past this point, use the code:

MEGNMIKE

	A	B	C	D
1	Axe			
2	Axe			Heart
3		Heart		
4	Potion	Potion		

Stage Two: Leap the pinkish plants before they can grab and hold you, and whip the Spiders before they send out little Spiders. Go down at the end; you'll get to the ledges above later. Make your way right, then climb; the last ledge on the left has Roast Beef. Don't forget to go right on the ledges too, though: there's a slew of Candles with a ton of Hearts. Get these, then climb up and off on the right.

Zombies rise from the ground, and your old Predatorlike semi-invisible friends are back. Also watch out for the Armadillo rolling in from the right. No real problems, however: even when you come to the Elevators, you *can* slog through the morass below, though it slows you down. After the Skeletal Knight, crack open the wall below the steps for Roast Beef. The next Elevator doesn't give you leeway for an error: miss and you die. Get off when it reaches top and cross the Bridge. The first Candle over the second section contains Roast Beef. Proceed slowly and you'll have no trouble with the Knights or Armadillo up ahead.

When you face the boss, Medusa, crouch when she uses her paralyzing glance and it'll miss you. Crouch, too, to kill the snakes she flings—though you may have to turn to kill any that she throws over your head. And though you've beaten the boss, the level's not over:

Thanks to an underground stream, stage 2–3 drags you along whether you want to go or not. The section begins with an attack of a Claw, then some Knights and a flying giant—one hit kills it, despite its formidable size!—and then the current changes directions after the fall, forcing you to the left. Leaping will get you ahead faster; just make sure you don't leap right into a monster or the deadly orange Spikes on top! After the next fall you speed up again, and so on. When you pass to the next area, a fireball-spitter awaits, so be ready to kill it. Ditto down below . . . with the additional problem that the current is carrying you away from it. Leap up between its fireballs in order to stay within whipping distance. Claws attack next, with another flying giant assault . . . then you're free! No boss to fight.

To get past this point, use the code:

MEGNMIKE

	A	B	C	D
1	Axe			Axe
2	Axe			Heart
3		Heart		
4	Heart	Potion		

Stage 3: Look out: the Spikes below mean instant death. Get across before the Ravens attack. The Stone Giants ahead don't die when hit: they break into Stone Midgets and attack. They split again, then finally perish when hit. After the first two Giants, there are two fire-breathing Dragonheads in a row. After the next set of Spikes is another Dragonhead: after you pass it, go down and to the *left*. Kill the Dragonhead there and break the wall beyond—without letting any of the upper Blocks fall on you. There's a veritable treasure trove of Candles, with Roast Beef at the end.

Go down, right, kill the Dragonhead, and get more Candles. Go right, fight the Stone Giants, leap the big Spike pit, fight the two Ravens, then watch out for falling Stalactites—and their pieces: they can hurt you as they bounce around. They quiver before they fall, but they're also hidden behind the status screen on top! Go slowly after these and there are no surprises.

The Bridge in the next selection collapses after a while, so don't dawdle; scoot under that orbiting ball of spikes and go ahead; you'll have to outrace it in just a moment! Climb after you whip the plant and keep going up: this is a vertical round. Just don't fall or it's instant death. (If you haven't perfected your Hook-swinging by now, you're in deep trouble.) Wherever possible, whip foes on overhead ledges by standing beneath them. Watch out for the Dragonhead hiding behind the second Waterfall halfway up. When you reach the Waterfalls on top, *don't* walk blindly ahead: there are ledges to be crossed here! Miss and you'll plummet to your death. Beyond, you'll see a ledge, over you, where there's a plant: kill it, then walk well out to the right: if you try to jump anywhere else, you'll hit your head on the ledge and fall! The rest isn't anything you haven't dealt with before. On the top left is a Watch, if you care to go for it. If not, exit right.

Next section: your foes will make a splash as they come rocketing up out of the water . . . even if there's a solid walkway ahead of you! Whip 'em as they appear, or they'll land and attack . . . and, rather rudely (and dangerously) spit a long stream of water at you. When you hop to the Candle ledge—and you must: it's the only sturdy one around—watch out: big falling objects will drop ahead of you. Let that happen: when they're done falling, rush ahead or the footing will fall apart beneath you. Stop on the ledge before the column—don't worry . . . it won't collapse—an Eyeball will attack from the right. Whip it from here. It's followed by a fireball-spitting fossil dinosaur that can be whipped into submission. Just hit its head six times: you'll be rewarded with a spinal column of Hearts! (Give it the sixth hit when all the vertebrae are extended so the Hearts will fall where you can reach them.)

Ascend and there's another dinosaur and an Eyeball. They're easy. The tough part is swinging on the Hook ahead: if you're attacked while crossing, don't stop—no kidding! Don't dawdle when you land: a squirter will appear and knock you back, killing you. Forge ahead! As soon as you land, crouch and kill the plant that springs up between the two Waterfalls. Next Hook: you'll have to jump and cast, or you'll never reach it. Climb and go left: get a Cross and obliterate your Skeletal foes. Use the Hook, continue left, Hook your way left again—if your Whip's too short, you'll have to step off the ledge and throw—then make your way to the stairs pronto: all the Blocks ahead will crack under your feet.

Upstairs: another dinosaur (no more Hearts!)

which you can kill from the ledge on the left. There's a Hook to the upper right, and a dinosaur above it, making life miserable for you. Swing across when the monster withdraws—landing carefully on the single stone, not the one with the monster on it—then jump across to the next ledge on the left. Make your way up the tower and, at the top, you'll battle the Orphic Vipers. The room floods and they emerge from the left, shooting flames and fireballs. Get on the ledge in the middle and attack the heads as they near; when the fireballs rocket up from under you, leap to get out of their way! One of the two heads will die when the meter is down to half; get the other by attacking from the very left edge of the ledge.

To get past this point, use the code:

MEGNMIKE

	A	B	C	D
1	Axe			Heart
2	Axe	Potion		Heart
3		Axe		Axe
4		Potion		

Stage Four: No trouble getting started: you're introduced to the green Trapdoors and the Claws that come from walls. You'll meet the first if you go past the stairs to the right; do so, though, because there's a big Heart if you shatter its wall.

Upstairs, go left, watching out for the Skeletons that hang down from the ceiling. When you reach the six Trapdoors—three top, three bottom—clear out the Candles below, return to the ledge, then jump onto and off of the first left ledge: if you linger even an *instant* you'll be dumped through the Trapdoor below it. Upstairs, hit up to kill the Skeletal Knight, then jump—again, *fast*—onto the right tip of the Trapdoor to go to the ex-Knight's ledge. There's Roast Beef over that Trapdoor: hit it when you're on top, jump down to get it, go from the Trapdoor to the lower right ledge, then repeat to go back up. (It's *really* tough—though possible—to jump from the top ledge to the Trapdoor, then get right back up again.)

Go right on top, watching out for the Raven when you cross the Trapdoors, then kneel on the ledge to kill the Knight. When you hit the Boss Puweyxil, the giant skull not only stabs at you with its tongue but causes deadly Coins to rain from the sky. Get on the low left ledge and kneel there. Attack the skull using Whip and weapons, and when it comes left, get under it and hit up. Puweyxil will protect you from the raining Coins! If you're not comfortable there, you can also go to the right at the boss from the ledge.

Finish him and you'll be in a room with a Hook: grab it and *hold on*, as the entire room turns ninety degrees. Get on the ledge and fight the Medusas, but don't go anywhere. When the room begins to tilt again, grab the Hook and hold on until a ledge forms on the left. Swing over to it. Cross the Logs and kill the Skeletons; no surprises here—except for the dazzling rotating background which serves no purpose other than to distract you. You can get a Cross and Roast Beef in this room.

The next room seems complicated but isn't. The floor sections rise and fall, often exposing Spikes. Go right and up—after the first Raven, before the first Spikes—then ride the floors up by shifting left and right to avoid being crushed. You can keep riding forever if you have a lot of time and need a lot of power-ups. If not, exit to the right when you see the Columns with the Spikes in front of them. There are three sets of Spikes here: the floor doesn't move, which is a good thing, since one touch of the Spikes will kill you. Make your way to the right. After clearing these, the floor will suddenly start rising *fast:* don't stop walking right, at a brisk clip, or you'll be crushed against new Spikes. You'll face the titanic boss Koranot here. Stand on the left ledge when it appears and toss Axes at him: you'll need at least 25. Even if you hit the monster's toe, it'll count—so keep heaving. He'll charge you, but just hold your ground, whipping and tossing. When he rises, get behind him and go to the ledge on the right. Repeat.

To get past this point, use the code:

MEGNMIKE

	A	B	C	D
1	Axe			
2	Axe			Heart
3		Heart		Axe
4	Potion	Heart		

Stage Five: Believe it or not, this one isn't nearly as difficult as the last two! Start by going right, up—fighting the Dragonhead on the right—and left, and fighting the second Dragonhead. A bird carrying a Gnome will attack moments later, from the left: get them before the Gnome drops, or it'll hop around and make a pest of itself. Another will follow in moments. And another. And another. At the top of the second slope is another Dragonhead. Go right, face the giant flying bug-thing, and when you face the two Dragonheads, get the lower one first; hit up to kill the second. Continue right, crossing the ledges quickly—you don't want to get knocked off by any airborne enemies.

A whipping Skeletal Knight greets you in stage 5–2. Attack it, or it'll box you in on the left. More follow, along with pesky Ravens, but they're easy enough to dispatch. Continue on to the room at the end and you're home free!

To get past this stage, use the password:

MEGNMIKE

	A	B	C	D
1	Axe			Axe
2	Axe	Potion		Heart
3		Axe		Axe
4	Potion	Heart		

Stage Six: You'll be better off leaping the Hounds as they attack here: they just keep coming back to life, and if you stand there whipping it, you're giving the Ghouls time to gather. Make your way to the right as quickly as possible—with an occasional leap to the left to get over a Hound. Get the Candle under the stairs first—a Raven will attack if you rush right up— and then climb. Leap off the top to the ledge on the right and then to the next ledge; kill the Raven that attacks from the right and drop down off the second ledge, crouching at the bottom. Whip right to the right to kill the Axe-throwing ogre—crouching will enable you to duck his Axes. *Don't* drop behind the bruiser: if you do, another will attack from the right, sandwiching you in. When the Axe-raiser is dead, go left and round up the goodies. Kneel to the left of the last ledge on the right and kill the Raven and the Axe-thrower. There are more Ghouls and Axe-tossers up ahead, but they won't trouble you. Careful, though: once again, their Axes survive their death *and* can get you coming and going. Fortunately, a whip-crack will destroy them.

Climb the stairs and allow yourself just a moment to look at the *dazzling* graphics of the swinging Chandelier to the left. Actually, there'll be four of them: you've got to go left, making your way across the gray platforms. There are ledges between them to give you a respite . . . and a Hook after the third one to make your life interesting. You don't get a second chance here: fall and you die, and it's back to the start of the Hound level! The *best* way to cross the Chandeliers is to get on the first of the four platforms when it's nearest, and jump to the second when the Chandelier is tilted with its right side *down*. Go to the next two when the left side is tilted down. When you're more comfortable with the Chandeliers, you'll be able to take two platforms at a time.

When you're through this room, you'll be in a chamber where the Chandeliers fall: you won't be hurt if you cross over them once they're down. However, if you start across before they've quite settled, a flying Candle may hit you. Treat these like the Stalactites back in Stage Three. After passing three of them, you'll face Ghosts that can only be made to vanish, for a moment, by whipping them. The Ectoplasm that circles amongst them should be ducked or jumped as you continue toward the left. Watch their patterns and make your way through.

There are Killer Coffins and more Skeletons beyond —only, like the Hounds, these boneheads don't stay dead when you whip them. Forge ahead, whipping the Tables that attack, and get the 1-Up from the wall over the Ledge on the right before facing the bosses. Bosses? Plural? Yes—you'll be facing Paula Abghoul and Fred Askare. They don't move in a predictable pattern, and now and then try to stab you with swords. Stay in the middle of the room and dodge out of their way, whipping them when you can. It isn't a good idea to go on the upper Ledges, where forward is the only way to escape the Dancing Specters!

To get past this level, use the code:

MEGNMIKE

	A	B	C	D
1	Axe			Heart
2	Axe	Heart		Heart
3		Potion		Potion
4		Heart		

Stage Seven: Make your way to the right: hit the Warriors from behind walls, ledges, or from below; there's plenty of time and it's relatively easy going. Go down the steps at the end of the area and watch out for both the flying demons—big targets, easy to knock out—and the Lamp Shades that attack suddenly and quickly: get in whipping line with them and hit them before they move. Continue going down. At the bottom (when the screen changes) head right—killing the two Warriors on the left—and cross using the floating Books. There are more troublesome Red Skeletons on the other side, so whip them before moving ahead.

The only surprises ahead: a Worm that, if you stay out of its way, will stay out of yours; and a Carpet that has a nasty habit of lifting up and carrying you with it . . . right into Spikes. Don't be standing when you go for a magic carpet ride! When you face the boss, Sir Grakul, stay on the left ledge and use your Whip and weapon, while leaping his armaments. He's surprisingly easy to beat.

To get past this stage, use the code:

MEGNMIKE

	A	B	C	D
1	Potion			Axe
2	Axe	Potion		Heart
3		Axe		Potion
4	Potion			

Stage Eight: Ah . . . nothing like a visit from old friends. You've got the Spider from Stage Two right off the bat—or should that be *bad*?—and then two falling Spikes which have to be crossed using expert timing. There's another Spider beyond; kill it fast or its little Spider will probably knock you back into the second Spike. The Green Drops falling up ahead are deadly, so avoid them. You've got a plant (easy) and a Dragonhead beyond; run right up to it, kill it—the Eyeball overhead won't get you if you're crouched at the foot of the steps, unless you take too long—then kill the Eyeball overhead. There's a second Dragonhead above and beyond—actually, you can get this one from below, whipping diagonally—followed by Spikes that swing like a pendulum. Cross underneath crouching . . . which will also enable you to kill the Warrior beyond. Spikes fall on you after that, but you want to get on top of them so you can cross ahead, leaping *over* the Spikes. An Eyeball will attack as soon as you land on the ledge: jump back to the left, onto the Spikes, and get down to the ground quickly on the left, whipping up while avoiding the Eyeball's fire. Get back up on the Spikes and continue on your way, crouching so you can kill the Dragonhead and another Eyeball beyond . . . and another Eyeball after that! Get on the Spikes and leap over the Dragonhead to the right: crouch, turn left, and kill it. You're under two Dragonheads now: whip up to kill the one on the left, then climb the stairs to do in the other.

Go upstairs and it's more of the same: pendulum Spikes followed by *regular* ones; jump on top of the latter one and, from there, leap on top of the next pendulum Spikes. Watch the next two Spikes carefully: go under both when the left one is just starting back up. The rest of this area is easily won using common sense as you move ahead cautiously.

Falling through the bad steps—either because you're clumsy or get knocked through—is the main problem of the next level, along with Bridges whose Blocks have a habit of disappearing. But, again, you can make it if you're careful.

The boss here is the Monster—that is, the Frankenstein Monster. Start on the left, whipping and using your weapons, then leap over him and hit at his back. You'll have to dodge the Monster's own fireballs; be prepared to take some hits.

Only skill is going to get you through the rest of the game. But if you want a peek at what lies ahead, use the code to face the level B boss Slogra:

MEGNMIKE

	A	B	C	D
1	Potion			Potion
2	Axe	Heart		Heart
3		Potion		Heart
4	Heart	Axe		

How to fight Slogra? The important thing to remember is that it leaps high off the screen when hit and loses its lance when its power is down to half. Start by staying in front of the Drape in the middle, hitting right as soon as Slogra has dropped from above. When you hit Slogra, it'll jump; rush to the right—to the left of the little column there—crouch, and hit left; rush *at once* to the left, crouch, and hit right when the creature lands; and so on. When its lance is gone, it'll attack with its pointy nose. Get on the column nearest you, crouch, hit the creature, then run to the opposite column.

When it's dead, you'll find two Roast Beefs outside the room.

The next monster is a grown-up version of the Zapf Bat you'll have fought earlier. Stay more or less in the center for the first half of the match. Whip up as the monster appears for the *second* time in the window, then keep whipping at it while it's aloft. When it lands, Spikes will fall from the ceiling; find a clear spot near you as they drop, then resume your attack. It'll begin firing eye beams, which can be avoided or deflected with a circular motion of your Whip. The monster will fall in a heap, momentarily stunned, when half its strength is gone: get near it and whip the heck out of it, since it becomes vulnerable again the instant it revives. When it's airborne again, play from side to side, *inside* the columns.

Next up—after a Roast Beef feast—the Grim Reaper. He forms from a slew of Reapers and flings mini-Scythes at you for the first half of the battle. If you've got time, stay in the lower left, to the left of the ledge, whipping up until the Reaper is half redead. *Don't budge* during that time: you're protected on three sides! Now . . . when the fiend's energy meter is half drained, he'll set down on the right. Go over . . . but beware! He has personal magnetism that will literally draw you to him. Whip when you're far enough away—pushing left on the pad is what's keeping you away from him, and you'll have to push right to whip him—and leap the large Scythe when he throws it to the left. (You'll probably only have to jump it once: the second throw is almost always over your head.) The Reaper will take to the air again then, but you shouldn't have any trouble getting in the last few hits now.

Finish here and Torches light your way to your last opponent: Dracula. If you want to go directly to the boss of bosses, use the following code:

MEGNMIKE

	A	B	C	D
1	Potion			Heart
2	Axe	Potion		Heart
3	Axe			
4		Axe	Axe	

When you reach the outside of the Castle and are facing Dracula's tower, *don't* go up the stairs. Not yet. Take a big leap to the left, over the moon, and you'll land on invisible steps! Walk to the lower left corner and you'll be rewarded with a full Heart Meter, Weapon, and Triple-Shot. When you're armed, walk back up the stairs but stop at the moon: there's a gap here, so you'll have to leap from the left cusp back to the platform. Climb the stairs and go left to face the Count.

The battle won't be easy: the vampire comes and goes in a long shaft of light, and is only vulnerable when he materializes for a few moments. Stay back and rely on your weapon until Dracula is weakened—the Boomerang is the weapon of choice here. Only then can you move in with the Whip. Beware, though: when Dracula begins to weaken, he summons a pair of devilish heads to attack you, and you'll not only be using your weapon and Whip, you'll be running, jumping, ducking, and darting like you never have before!

Rating: A

Challenge: A

Tough game! There are new twists, but all of the qualities that made the series great are here as well.

Graphics: A

From the marvelous password, which you

carve in stone, to the animation to the three-dimensional scenery, this one's a complete winner!

Sound Effects: A

The music is very good (though it's no *Act-Raiser*), but the sound effects are top-notch.

Simulation: A

The Whip is incredibly life-like, as are the hero's moves. And when the room turns in Stage Four, you'll definitely feel it . . . !

ghoul bar go abble to the is world on the... wrong direct that scene... to rescued t 17... only place

SUPER GHOULS 'N GHOSTS

Type: Fantasy quest

Objective: Once before, Arthur saved Princess Guinevere and the realm. Now, the evil Sardius has taken Guinevere to the Phantom Zone—no, not the same one where Kryptonian villains are sent—the denizens of the Ghoul Realm have returned, and Arthur is once again out to destroy villainy and rescue Guinevere.

Heroes: Arthur can run, jump, and acquire various weapons as described in the instruction booklet. These appear in Chests, and are different from game to game—though the Chests appear in the same places. Be careful: some Chests hold damaging items like Bear Traps or enchantment that'll turn you into a crawling baby. Look before you step! In his basic armor, Arthur can take one hit from a foe and, though it'll knock the armor off, he'll survive. A second hit will kill him.

Enemies: Ghouls and monsters of all kinds; these are plentiful, and will be described in *Strategies* as you encounter them.

Menu: The game is for one player only. You can change the button layout to suit your own taste, however.

Scoring: You earn points for killing enemies and collecting Gold. You play against a timer.

Strategies: Here's the quest-by-quest lowdown:

Quest 1: The Dead Place

The Haunted Graveyard: Kill the Zombies, get on the stone, and collect the Chest. Wait until the Prison is exposed, enter, and kill the Flamethrower; if you go across the top, you'll have to fight the Hound *and* the fire demon, who can shoot up at you. Open the Chest beyond and watch out for more Flamethrowers and Hounds. At the third Prison, go through it, kill the Flamethrower, then go up and get the Chest on the roof. The Demon Totems up ahead drop Skulls on you, so be careful. Hop across the water, staying put during the Tidal Waves. Be ready to leap the Pearls that a giant Clam will be spitting from the right.

The Forest of Fear: Move slowly: Flaming Skulls roll down at you and have to be jumped, not slain. Look out for the giant—what, Raspberries?—that grow ahead and move slowly to and fro. And don't get complacent just because Skulls are lying on flat ground: this place *is* susceptible to earthquakes! When the Boss arrives, watch out—this Bird has an extendable neck *and* spits Eggs that hatch into little Birds. Just keep shooting at its head, blasting the Eggs before they hatch, and staying as far to the left as you can.

Quest 2: The Rotting Sea

The Graveyard of Ships: Move quickly, even off the pier: everything in this level is sinking slowly! Make

124

your way across and then up the Mast, steering clear of Ghosts—harmless in their small, gray form but dangerous when they grow and whiten—and ducking Pendulums. Ride the rig over to the Mast on the right, climb, and continue to the next Mast on the right. When you reach the bow of the ship, double-jump to the hanging Raft and ride into—

The Sea of Despair: You'll have to leap from Raft to Raft to Reef, creaming the Flying Piranhas that come from the right, and timing your forward motion so you can ride the raft on the swells *over* the Spiny Coral or through sections where there are no Spines or areas where they can be shot off. (If you happen to get nicked here, take advantage of it: remember, you're invulnerable for a few moments after you've been hurt. Use that time to pass through.) Some of the Coral also has deadly, projectile-spitting Anemones clinging to them: don't proceed until you've shot these dead. Toward the end you'll face Fish that swim up from the bottom and attack, *Jaws*like. When you're through this region, a supergiant Coral attacks, hurling little Squids at you. When the giant moves out from the Waterfall, stay to the left, firing at its face; touching any part of it will kill you. If you can't kill the Squids, leap them; they won't come back.

Quest 3: Vermilion Horror

Crucible of Flame: Make your way down the Ladders, watching out for the Fire Babies and the flame-breathing brutes below—you can destroy their fireballs with your weapon. Be very careful, too, about standing under those Gargoyles in the Ledges: now and then Lava comes pouring from the mouths of these grinning fiends. (Note: if you happen to touch or land in Lava while you're wearing armor, you can wade out if you *hustle*!) When you reach the Lava Flow below, wait for the Rock Columns to rise up before attempting to cross. Use the stone Elevators to bring you to more Columns. When you reach solid ground again, move right while firing your weapon: there's a bat-thing beyond, so be ready to fight it. It'll hover out of reach and drop projectiles if you don't kill it quickly. If you don't kill it at all, it will dog you as you enter—

Towers of Molten Steel: You'll come to a Tower with an up-rising spiral ramp and you'll have to kill Gargoyles and Bats as you make your way through here. Ascend the tower slowly to the floating Ledge on the right. Cross to the next Tower—which has a horizontal ramp—to the floating Ledge beyond. There's another spiral Tower, then a horizontal one, then a spiral Tower leading down. Cross the Ledges beyond and stop on the Ledge to the immediate left of the Keyhole. Face left: the boss—a fanged Worm—will arrive and circle you counterclockwise. Fire left first, then right, and so on as it orbits you. You will be safe, here, from its projectiles. Stay put, crouching all the while, and you won't be hurt.

Quest 4: The Ghoul's Stomach

Nice-sounding place to visit, eh? Well, it's even more disgusting than that. Flying blue Ogres rise up: kill them quickly and move right. If you delay here, the ground below your feet will turn to mush and you'll sink to your death. Get to the Ledge quickly and stay there: the whole world turns around you. Go left from the first Ledge—watching out for the green-flaming snake-thing (what would *you* call it?) that uncoils above and spits fireballs—then get on the next Ledge quickly and go right when the world comes to a rest. Kill the next green-flaming snake-thing, climb up on the right, jump to the left—killing your serpentine friend on the upper left—and go left (ignore the

Ledge on the upper right). Lots of Gold along this corridor, but watch those double jumps or you may end up hitting the overhead Spikes. Get on the Ledge at the end, then go left, double-jumping over the Spikes. Get on the next Ledge, go left, and you're outta there! You'll magically materialize on a Ledge that tilts a bit but is relatively easy to ride. You'll have to shift right and left as Steam vents from above, and there are blue Raspberries here that need to be shot as you proceed—guess they weren't Raspberries after all, though they sure do look like 'em. Double-jump to the next Ledge, and as you climb, watch out for the same kind of Fire Babies that rose from the Lava in the last level. You'll be drifting to the right now; at the end of your trip, climb and you'll ride to the left. Just when it looks like you can't go anywhere else, you'll be spirited to the boss. The three-headed Dragon is surprisingly easy to slay: just keep firing to the right, at its heads. When it dies, though, it doesn't really: a Baby Dragon emerges and, if you don't kill it quickly, grows into a new Dragon.

Quest 5: The Deep Chill

Ice Forest: There's a bizzard blowin'! Watch out for the Ogres ahead—their frigid breath is lethal—and the deadly Icicles, which are stationary but must be leapt or ducked. A flower above you fires deadly spores: destroy it and climb the giant Tree you're on. More Ogres, more Flowers, and when you reach solid ground above, be very careful: Ice Roots grow from the ground, blocking your path—at least they make a groaning sound and disturb the snow, alerting you before they rise; shoot them to shatter them. After the first Roots, flying, frozen Knights weave up and down from the right. *Don't* rush ahead to kill them: more Roots will rise and skewer you. Rather, back up a little, take out the Knights, then get to the root of the

Roots. Cross this region slowly, as Knights and Roots are plentiful. Cross the Ice Bridge before it shatters and get set for—

Ice Wall: Kill the Hounds, go right, then up, then right. At the Ice Bridge ahead, wait by the Ladder: the first Cloud comes along, and you won't be able to see where you're going. More Clouds follow, so proceed slowly: for the moment that you're blind, you could be attacked! When the Ice Demon attacks you, just stay to the left, shoot at its head, and duck the Ice Claws it throws.

Quest 6: The Castle of the Emperor

Kill the baby Demons on the Ladder, then double-jump to execute the Bird on the left. Go up and repeat by killing the Bird on the right. Go up, climb the Ladder, and kill the next Bird, also on the right. All the while, the little blue devils will attack you. If you've got the time, drop down to the bottom, where you have some maneuvering room; they'll usually follow you. In any case, as soon as they appear, go to the opposite side of the Ledge and attack. Go right at the top: the Chest there *usually* contains evil! Watch out for the flying Demon beyond—Crossbow is the best way to nail the critter—then climb the Ladder.

Quest 7: Hallway of Ghouls

There are two Birds on top, on opposite ends of the screen, spitting fireballs; stand under the blue window and take out the one on the right before scrolling on the left one—though a fireball or two may drift down from the upper left. Turn left and kill that one, then go left when they're both fricasseed. The columns ahead will disintegrate as you approach, allowing you to climb the steps to the next Ladder. There are Ghosts at the top: don't let them stop you from climbing the sloping Ledges—and getting to the Chests thereupon. At the top, leap to the Ladder, drop down off the right side, and go right. The big brute at the end fires fireballs followed by Lasers: stay on the left and just keep jumping up at its head. When you win here, bad news awaits. Guinevere appears and tells you you've got to go back to the beginning of the game, explore all the Chests, and find the magic Bracelet—the only weapon powerful enough to destroy Sardius. So, of course you go. When you get back here and win, it's time for—

Quest 8: The Throne Room

What can you say about Sardius? He's big and powerful, but thoughtful. He spits out two Discs that you can use to ride to his head. Get up there, fire away, avoid his own projectiles, get down, jump on a new Disc, and fire some more! If you haven't got the Bracelet's power, don't bother. However, there *is* a way you can get a look at the fiend and scope out his lair before the final battle. In fact, you can have a look at every one of the game's quests as follows:

To execute stage select, plug in controller one and two—Nintendo's own controllers; other ones may not work. Use controller one to go to the Option screen. There, move the cursor to Exit. On controller two, press the left button and start; while holding those two down, hit start on controller one. That will bring you to an options screen, where you can make your choice.

Rating: B+

    Challenge: A

        From the little monsters to big, from earthquakes to tsunamis, this game's got it all!

    Graphics: B

The animation's a little jerky, but the scenery is spooktacular!

Sound Effects: C

Evocative if unspectacular music; predictable, unspectacular sounds.

Simulation: A

You'll feel the power of the weapons, and you'll actually feel a little weightless doing those double-jumps!

SUPER MARIO WORLD

Type: Fantasy shoot-'em-up

Objective: While vacationing in Dinosaur Land, Mario and Luigi are shocked by the abduction of Princess Toadstool. While searching for her, they befriend the young dinosaur Yoshi, who tells the brothers how all of the dinosaurs were sealed in Eggs by evil Turtles. *Turtles?* That can only mean Bowser has returned . . . and has the Princess!

Heroes: What *can't* Mario, Luigi, and Yoshi do in this game? Practically nothing! Mario and Luigi can walk, jump, spin-jump, swim, hold or punch certain things, fly (with a Cape), and throw fireballs. Yoshi can walk and fly. Mario/Luigi can also collect power-up items and Coins, the latter adding a life when they've got enough of them. Each character can have a maximum of 99 lives.

Enemies: These are plentiful and are described as they're encountered in *Strategies*, below.

Menu: One or two players can search for the Princess alternately.

Scoring: Mario earns points for every enemy bopped and for power-ups acquired. The player races against a timer.

Strategies: From start to finish, here's what to look for, what to avoid, and how to survive!

Yoshi's Island 1: Don't be intimidated by the big bullet, Banzai Bill. You can duck into the pits *or* leap up and bop him. One hit will do it. After the first Jumping Piranha Plant, you'll find a Pipe surrounded by Blocks. Spin-jump the golden Blocks to break them, and enter the Pipe for bonuses. Exit, and when you reach the Cloud Blocks, hit the golden Block to the left for a 1-Up. Chase it to the right. Way above the Clouds, to the left, are Clouds that are presently out of sight; you'll be returning to this region later. Continue right, and when you reach the Uprights, hit the bar when it's high; the higher it is, the greater the bonus you'll receive.

Yoshi's Island 2: Pick up the Shell and use it to bowl down the Koopa Troopas ahead. Hit the Block at the end of the second Plateau and Yoshi will appear. Get on the dinosaur's back and press on. When you get the Cape, you can earn a virtually limitless supply of 1-Ups using the Shell right before the steps. Spin the Shell against the steps and, when it bounces back, Spin at it again. Keep it up and watch your 1-Ups grow! After the three ? Blocks—with the 1-Up in the middle—beware the Monty Moles that pop from the side of the next set of Plateaus. When you reach the two Blocks beside the Plateau, hit the one on the right to cause a Vine to sprout. Climb to Coins in the sky. After the next Plateaus, enter the Pipe and get the flying ?'s by jumping Yoshi and, while the dinosaur's aloft, spin-jumping off its back. Exit.

Yoshi's Island 3: Go to the top of the Mountain and cross to the right. The ledges ahead swing 'round in a clockwise motion. You won't fall off, but don't jump forward until you're back at the twelve or one o'clock position. The next set of Ledges are made up of Blocks that fold, accordionlike, into the center Block: if you're not on that Block, you may be dumped down. You've only got a second to get to the center if you land on one of the outer Blocks. The first time you cross here, you *want* to drop: fall, go left, and jump up under the ! Blocks for Mushroom after Mushroom—something you can only do if you've got Yoshi. Otherwise, you won't be able to get the height you need. (If you haven't got a Yoshi, go right on top and get one from the right ? ahead.) Leap onto the ! Block on the far left, against the Mountain after you've got the prize from that one, then go back up and continue right. Go down the first Pipe—only visible after you cross the solid Ledges and the Plateau beyond, and get on the rotating Ledge and ride it down. Collect the lower Coins *only*, then use the P Switch to transform the rest into a bridge. Collect the Dragon Coin on the other side and exit. No surprises after this: if you drop down at the first accordion Ledges, you'll land on a fortune of ! Blocks. Tap them as you go forward.

Yoshi's Island 4: Watch out for the Islands here: they sink. Rush ahead so the Blurps don't get you. Stay down here, by the waters, crossing Islands to the right. Enter the first Pipe if you feel like facing Pokeys. If you've got Yoshi, let the dinosaur eat the cactus creatures. If not, run and leap them and use the Blocks above to get over them. When you exit the Pipe, apart from getting a Super Star in the Block to the left, pick up the Shell and throw it up, at the Block. Jump Yoshi and spin-jump up to collect the goodies. Ahead, beware Floating Mines that pass by the Islands. If you got the Super Star, you should be able to race to the very end of the level without stopping.

Iggy's Castle: Climb the Fence when necessary: the Koopas on the other side can't get you when you're there—though you can get them by punching; eight felled Koopas earns you a 1-Up. Defeat the Koopas on your side by stepping down on them. When you reach the P, hit it as Super Mario and you'll get firepower from the middle ? above. Beware the Lava Bubbles as you cross the bubbling pits. Next section: *don't rush ahead for the Coins!* Columns come down and will crush you if you're under them. Though the screen scrolls by itself, wait until the first Column has come down and risen before going ahead. Don't stop, but continue past the small Pit; you'll clear the next Column, no sweat. Watch for the flying ? here, then wait for the next Column; rush past, then run over the accordion Ledge before the last Column comes crashing down. When you pass through the door at the end, you'll find youself on an inverted Shell with Iggy Koopa. Stomp him—watching out for his fireballs—stay on the "up" side of the Shell and bop Iggy repeatedly down the slope to knock him into the steamy drink. When he falls off the Shell, the round is over.

Donut Plains

Donut Plains 1: The Super Koopa that comes along is wearing a Cape: stomp it, claim the Cape, and take off! (You can't get a cape from *every* Super Koopa here, so try and get it right the first time!) After collecting Coins up above, you'll come to a third bank of Clouds: land and enter the downfacing Pipe to your left—just jump right up into it. If you come down before the Pipe, watch out for the Baseball-throwing

Chargin' Chuck you'll encounter. Inside the Pipe, hit the ?'s and exit. You can get just Coins in here . . . or, if you're really lucky, you can get three 1-Ups and more! If you lost your Yoshi, get one in the ? over the Plateau up ahead. Go left from the Plateau and enter the upward-facing Pipe to the left of the downward-facing Pipe. Leave Yoshi behind and walk right up the Pipe; fly ahead and literally sweep up the Coins. Exit using the Pipe at the far right. Continue right, and after the Plateau, bop the Chargin' Chucks so you can get a 1-Up from the solo Block there. The rightmost Block sticking out from the Plateau (to your left) will sprout a Vine which will enable you to get a Dragon Coin from above. If there's a wall up ahead, run up the Blocks. If not, fly up. You'll find a Key on the upper Ledge: use it to enter—

Donut Secret 1: Or is this the mysterious Water World from Super Mario Bros? Collect all the power-ups, watching out for the Blurps who live here. Enter the Pipe and hit the first ? for a Power Balloon. Float around, collecting Coins and power-ups, watching out for the Winged Koopa Troopas; if you went straight up, then the P Switch to the left will give you another Balloon so you can continue to float. Important: if you can get a Shell here, bring it back to the Water World when you return. Drop it into the pit where the Dragon Coin is, and you'll get plenty of 1-Ups. Anyway—continue through the water and get the P Switch near the end. *Don't* use it there: bring it ahead to the row of Blocks by the Keyhole and use it there to expose the Key—last Block on the right. Enter—

Donut Secret House: Go up the stairs, right, down, and right under the wall. Enter the door at the end and go left. Past the door is a P: take it right and up to the locked door. Enter and fight Big Boo, knocking him out with three thrown Blocks. When the hefty ghost dies, you're out of there. Take other paths and you'll find yourself repeating routes endlessly—though you'll be able to pick up a lot of Coins and such.

Donut Plains 2: The screen scrolls like it did just before you fought Iggy, and Columns rise and fall like before. This time, however, you can ride the Columns up and down, as long as you're in a nook or cranny where you won't get crushed. Enter the second, smaller of the *green* Pipes up ahead. Climb the Blocks; the last will sprout a Vine and enable you to climb to a Key. (Use the Shell, ahead, to hit up at the Block.) Go to the Green Switch Palace and then make your way to—

Donut Ghost House: If you can't fly, go right, enter the door, hit up under the Block, jump to the stairs, and climb the Vine. Enter the door and exit. If you *can* fly, do so: fly up and cross on the top. At the end of the room, hit the first and second Blocks first, to get 1-Ups; then hit the third and fourth for two more. More important: reenter the Ghost House, run to the right, turn, and zoom to the left so you can fly. Take off and land on the floor above, go all the way to the right, and drop off the side. You'll find a door at the bottom: enter. When you're back on the map screen, go straight up and you'll be in a Top Secret Area chock full of power-ups and Yoshi! Go back here whenever your powers are at a low.

Donut Plains 3: Rotating Ledges and Ledges on Wires drawn by Pulleys greet you here—you can stand on the hub of the rotating Ledges, by the way. Bugging you as you go are Koopas—though there aren't that many, nor will they present a problem. When you reach the Plateau with the two Coin ?'s, be certain to fly up to the Clouds and the wealth of Coins to be found there. (No Wings? Let Yoshi dine on the blue Koopa, then hit the B button. Or, even easier: hit the rightmost Block of the row and a Vine will sprout.) When you descend, don't bother backtracking: you didn't miss a thing on the ground! If you couldn't fly, cross the Plateaus. When you reach the first Pulley Ledge with an On/Off Block, change it so you can continue. Hit the next On/Off Block as well: stand in the front of the Ledge so that there's something to land on when you come down! In the second section on this level, you'll be bothered mostly by Fuzzies. Up ahead are a rotating Ledge—with three Ledges— followed by three Pulley Ledges on top and three flat ones below. Take the Pulley Ledges—even though the Wire ends, the Ledges will jump; all you have to do is jump when they do—and enter the Pipe up ahead. (If you want to try a more daring entry, go to the right of the Pipe and the rotating Ledge there: hop to the left, springing off the back of a Paratroopa into the opening.) Inside the Pipe, hit the ?'s—you can get three 1-Ups here, if you're lucky—and make your way to the top. Exit and go right on the Rotating Ledge; no surprises to the end.

Donut Plains 4: Hit the ground running with your finger on the X button: you've got to race to the Shell on the right and boot it before the Koopa puts it on. The green Pipes rise and fall here; make sure, as with the first one, that you bop the Koopa first, or you may find your way barred with the creature coming back at you! *Don't* enter the fourth Pipe: it leads to a world of rising and falling Pipes and nettlesome Koopas. Watch out for the Hammer Brother after you cross the pit with the green Pipe on its right side: he'll attack after you pass the gray Pipe. Run under him and jump up against his perch to knock him off. Get on the rock and leap to the perch to ride up to the Plateau—all of this assumes you don't have flight. There'll be a small army of Koopas and and Goombas up ahead: bash the Koopa on the downward-facing slope ahead and let its Shell knock down the others. The next Pipe is worth entering for the Coins; even if you aren't powered-up at all, you can cross the pit at the end by leaping across the row of Winged Koopa Troopas! When you exit, you'll literally be fired from the mouth of the Cannon, right over the head of the awful Hammer Brother, to the end of this section. If you have a Cape, be sure to fly up to the hidden Clouds here: hit the Block on top to get a 1-Up. In the second section the first Block will give you Yoshi. The Block after the Dragon Coin will give you the power-up you want if you hit it at the right time—that is, while it's on the symbol *before* the one you want to get. It's recommended that you get the Cape if you don't have one: fly up—over the Para-Goombas—and visit the Clouds ahead. There's a 3-Up Moon on top! (You can also get up there with Yoshi, if he manages to dine on a blue Shell.) Regardless, the rest of this region is a piece of cake!

Donut Secret 2: Regardless of the order in which you took Donut Secret 1 and Donut Secret House, you've got to go through here before you can finish up the Donut Plains. Go over the Ice Mountain ahead and use the Jumping Board to hit the Block. A Vine will sprout: climb to the Ice Ledge above and get the Super Star from the Block above. Jump down to the right and charge ahead, entering the downward-facing Pipe that follows the three on the ground. Inside, get the P Balloon and float through the Coin field. Exit —you'll drop down when you emerge—and get the

Super Star from the first Block you encounter. Cross to the sloping Mountain ahead and get to the top of the one beyond it: bop the Paratroopas there, and after you've defeated them all, press right for a 1-Up.

Morton's Castle

Beware the pair of Thwimps that drop down as soon as you enter here, then hop back and forth to try and pulverize you. If you can fly straight up, spare yourself some agony—and earn some bonuses—by soaring up to the Pipe above. If not, go up the sloping wall—which moves ahead whether you like it or not! —ducking the trio of Ball 'N' Chains and making your way through the door. On the other side, go left —but not recklessly. Thwomps fall here; watch their expression. When they show teeth, it means they're coming down! Wait until they drop and are on the rise again before you proceed. Lava Bubbles rise from the pit above, so you don't want to go leaping across until after one is on the way down. Stop on the step across the Pit and wait for another Thwomp to fall. Continue, kill the Dry Bones, and exit.

The next section is an uphill battle, literally: you've got to climb to the top of the Castle tower. Problem is, the Blocks you've got to climb don't stay put, so move with an eye on where you can plant your feet up ahead. Go right, climb the stairs when they appear, and stand on the thin wall on the right. Jump left, hop to the next level on the left, and cross to the right, where the three ?'s are. When the Block under them is starting left, slip under the ?'s and hit them; the center ? has a power-up. Don't stay any longer than you have to, naturally, since that Block is headin' back! Get up on the former ?'s, hop right when the Block comes from the wall, and leap left. Get up onto the gray Blocks quickly, then onto the gray wall in the center. Wait on the Block to their right and jump right when the Block appears. Hop left to the Block with the Jumping Board guarded by a Dry Bones. Bop the Bones and carry the Jumping Board to the right; use it to vault up into the Coin room, then take it back to the left and use it to leap up. Wait until the steps appear on the left, then jump and knock into the Blocks with the Dry Bones on top. The monster will plummet to its death and you can continue up through the Blocks to the right. Climb the light-gray Blocks along the left —quickly, lest the Blocks moving from the right mash you—until you reach the next three ?'s guarded by a trio of Dry Bones. After uncovering the goodies, use the middle Block to jump up. Go up the right side, leaping with care to the left, next, from Column to Column, since you don't want to drop onto the Spikes. Stop on the second one from the left and jump up when the Block appears; the way to the door is up past the Dry Bones.

Now you're in Morton's room, and he doesn't want you there! All it takes is three bops on the head to kill him. Now, he climbs walls: if you jump on his face, you accomplish nothing. When he climbs, he's headed for the ceiling and is going to drop down: stay in the center of the room and, when he reaches the ceiling and stops, Y button yourself quickly in the opposite direction. He'll fall more or less straight down and miss you.

Vanilla Dome

Vanilla Dome 1: Your first foe, ambling up the stairs, is a Spike Top. Spin-jump to kill it. Swoopers swoop next. Let the first blue Shell Koopa walk off the cliff, get the power-up from the flying ?, then continue ahead, but *stay on the ground*. When you reach the Block structure, don't go near it: you won't be able to get out! Wait for the blue Shell Koopa, bop it, take its Shell, and Y-run forward on the ground. Use the Shell to knock off the next two Koopas and continue ahead. (If you only nail one, you'll be in a fix since you'll have to jump up . . . and you'll get caught in the Blocks.) Enter the last Block room only, for the power-up; you can get out by going up and right and dropping down. Before going to the top, though, hit the leftmost overhead Block for a 1-Up. At the ?, bop the Koopa and throw its Shell against it to get the power-up. Climb the stairs, hit the Block for a Vine, and ascend—spin-jumping off Yoshi—to get the Key that will allow you into the Secret areas of this realm.

Next section: hit the ?, get the Super Star, and Y-button *race* your little legs off to keep from being swallowed up: the ground is sinking at an alarming rate into the Lava! Leaping will help get you through here even quicker. When you're clear, go through the Pipe, leap the Uprights, and jump at the Coins. Don't worry: there's land below, even though you can't see it. The Koopas are easily dispatched, but don't go bowling with Shells: they will almost certainly ricochet off the walls ahead and mow you down! When you reach the two Blocks, hit one and jump up onto the next. Go right, time your moves past the Spike Tops—or destroy them, if you're in that kind of mood —and get a power-up from the ? ahead, keeping in mind that it may just drift to the right . . . Cross the Pipes; if there're no Blocks between them, hop on the Winged Koopa's back to get across. To get up the steep slope, keep the pad pressed right and B button up. Get the Coins below, jump the Pit, and continue on the bottom—being careful not to toss the Shell into the Block on the right, or it'll bounce back at you. Get the Dragon Coin at the end, then double back and hop up through the two Blocks. Go right, carrying one of the Shells so you can hit you-know-who up ahead ready to punt a Football in your general direction!

Vanilla Dome 2: You start in water, so swim right and nail the Blurp ahead. Cross the land, go for a dip, and swim under the ?'s to get the Coins and power-up. Remembering that Koopas can swim, dog paddle right, keeping a careful eye on the Blurps. Don't sink down into the Pit; hit the ? ahead and expose a Vine. Climb to dry land. When you see the Koopa in a Pit, hit it so it's far left or right and you have a place to step off. Otherwise, it'll keep bouncing back and forth and kill you. Drop back into the water when you reach the Coins—they form a cute little arrow pointing down—swim right, and collect the goodies from the ?, including the 1-Up from the invisible Block at the left. Swimming right, you'll get another power-up on the right side of the wall. Leave the water there, climb the slope, and continue right. There'll be a pair of Chargin' Chucks after that, followed by a Block where you can choose your own power-up. Another Chuck and a P Switch are next: don't use it here, but carry it to the wall of Blocks back to the left. Race ahead, through these Coins and through the Coins to the left of where you saw that arrow before. Drop down in the water, swim left, and get the Key—to the left of the Dragon Coin. Swim right, drop down, swim left, and use the Key. In case you messed up with the P Switch, continue right and enter the green Pipe ahead. You'll be in an ice zone where you slide considerably in whatever direction you're moving. Emerge and you face a slew of Swoopers *at once* and a trio of Chucks moments later. Pass them and you're out of there!

Vanilla Ghost House: Eeries welcome you, followed by Circling Boo Buddies. The ? in their midst contains a power-up. Leap the Ledges, avoiding the various specters trying to kill you. When you reach the Blocks, stay under the lower row and hit the third

Block in the section to the right—that is (how appropriate!) the thirteenth from the left. Go right and up to the top level and climb to avoid the Big Blue Boo that will give chase. Don't climb to the small Ledge on top, but go right on the one below it. You'll easily jump to Eeries; drop down at the end and exit. Next section: time your moves to avoid the Big Bubbles by retreating to the left or rushing ahead, as necessary. But that's not the difficult part. When you reach the P Switch, pick it up and carry it to the quintet of Coins that look like a door. Actually, they *are* a door, but you can't open it unless you use the P here. First, however, clear out some of the Coins so there's enough room for Mario to exit. (You *don't* want to use the first door you encounter: it'll take you way back in the previous section.)

Vanilla Dome 3: Yes, you can ride the Skull Raft at your feet. Just stay hoppin' as you go, because Blargg will rise up beneath you even before you reach the ?. Yoshi can eat the big Lava hippo. Otherwise, stay on the very right of the Raft and jump it. Leap on the first flying ?, jump from it to the stationary ?, then jump from that up against the next flying ?, which has a 1-Up. If you've timed it right, it'll fall when your Raft is passing underneath. Jump the second Blargg, stomp the Koopa headed your way when you reach the shore, and use the edge of the gold Pipe if you must in order to reach the ? and get its power-up. Deal with the Piranhas in the Pipes just as you did the Jumping Piranha Plants. After the slope down, wait at the bottom for a flying ?, then get on the Raft. Nothing will happen till you're on top of the Lava river, when three Blarggs in a row will attack. Jump them exactly as before, from the right side of the Raft. When the Raft falls off the side, it'll do so in pieces: just stay put on one of them. The Raft will reassemble at the bottom! If you've got a Cape, fly up to the left for the 3-Up Moon in the niche there. (Fly off and into a Pit below and you can come back and collect more, with an aggregate gain of two lives each time.) When you reach the Pipe, jump up on its left side to uncover an invisible Block. After the Pipes, fly up to the right to enter a Pipe that leads to a secret ? room. If you can't get up there, make your way past the five downward-facing Pipes, timing your moves to take you past the Piranhas in one, two, and four. (Truth is, if you just run right through here as soon as you arrive, and don't stop, none of them will get you.) Hop onto the Raft to get to the Ledge above the Lava, head right, and use the Koopa's Shell to kill the Piranha ahead—*why* did they make these things look like pumpkins? Sail the Raft over to the gold Pipe and enter. (Raft gone? Go back to the left and get another.) Oh, good: more ice. Deal with it as before. When you get outside—

Go to the Pipe, then double back to the left to cause the Shell to sit still. Go over the Pipe—using Y while pressing right on the pad, if you don't have a Cape—and collect the items from the Blocks overhead. Ride the Raft over the four Blargs in a row—going to the Ledge overhead for the Dragon Coin as you go over the Falls, if you feel up to it—then leave the Raft and head right, past the Spike Tops (there's nothing in the Pipes), across the Ledges, and to the ? with its power-up. If you can fly, do so to the upper right. No surprises for the rest of the level, bottom or top.

Vanilla Dome 4: This is pretty straightforward: some wicked birds flying overhead, and Koopa Marios, but no new twists. The challenge here is to make it through without your Cape, since there isn't really any "elbow room" top or bottom. You'll be using the green Springboard Ledges to get through: jump off the Koopa's Mario head at the end to break the tape between the Uprights. Enter the *second* Pipe at the end —Yoshi can't get through the bonus area—and have fun with the Lava "bonus" level. No monsters here, just plenty of Coins. *However*: there are walls to jump. If Mario doesn't clear these in time to get back on the Raft, it's oblivion. Press on when you exit. Again, it's all timing here, and you'll come to recognize the patterns very quickly.

Lemmy's Castle: Your pals the rotating Blocks are back, along with Magikoopas. Get down to the bottom level by waiting for a Magikoopa spell to hit one of the Blocks and spin it. Go right. Eventually you'll come to a door: it's opened, of course, by the P Switch that was above you to the left, three Ledges back. Bring it below the door, snatch the three Coins on the side, and hit the P: you can get into a 1-Up room. If you mess up, continue right and take the door at the end of the room—which is where the 1-Up room would've left you off. More shifting Blocks and Ledges here, as in Morton's Castle—only this time it's horizontal. And there's Lava waiting to smother you if you do the wrong thing. When you reach the end of this ordeal, you'll find that beating Lemmy is a cinch. Though there are two fake Lemmies, all you have to do is crouch on the top of the Pipe on the far right. The genuine article will emerge from that one, and you'll have no trouble stomping him thrice.

Vanilla Secret 1: Using Jumping Ledges and climbing, you've got to make your way up this long vertical chamber. The trick here, again, is in the timing: at one point you've got to use a Jumping Board to fire yourself up through a row of Koopas with only a narrow space between them—unless, of course, you had the wisdom to pick up Shells and toss them up at these dudes to widen the gap! Two points to remember: over the horizontal green Pipe, the middle Block gives you a Vine; the Block to the left of the Vine gives you another one so you can continue climbing.

Vanilla Secret 2: Welcome back, Yoshi! The first ? gives you the dinosaur; use a Koopa Shell—do these look like Ernie Kovacs, or is it me?—to hit the ! and get a power-up. (If you've got a Cape, fly and visit the sky full of Coins.) On the ground, oodles of Koopas await. They leap high and low; you'll recognize the patterns after a few times. Jump from head to head or jump over one, run under the next, and so on—which you can do throughout most of the Koopa phase of this level. When you reach the slope, let the Spiny fall before you continue, then get under the Note Blocks: the third from the left will give you a power-up. Unlike the Piranha Plants, the Lakitu in a Pipe here and ahead can be killed by jumping on it. Watch out for the Parabombs as you continue; up ahead, enter the second Pipe with the Lakitu in a Pipe. After you clear this area, you'll be Cannon-shot to the end.

Vanilla Secret 3: Use the friendly Dolphins here as Ledges, only don't expect *all* of them to go to the right! The ? above has a power-up; the Dolphins here are all swimming to the left, so make sure none of them carries you off as they whisk by. If you ride this herd to the right, you'll have to race against the wind, as it were, taking huge leaps off their backs. If you have to take a dip, don't worry: no foes here . . . Yet. After the next Plateau is a Porcupuffer. The fish'll chase you—even if you stay on the Plateau to the left, Porcupuffer will come running—so stay aloft. You can use the nose of the vertically leaping Dolphin if you need a perch. Porcupuffer will keep chasing you after the next plateau. If you end up in the water, don't swim, but *leap* ahead or you'll be caught. The next area is very straightforward: leap from nose to nose and go right.

Vanilla Fortress: Ball 'N' Chains tax you, followed by a Spiked Ledge: better to be normal Mario here, since you can pass easily under everything. (If you *aren't* normal when you start, you will be after getting clobbered or poked!) Pass under the Spikes and enter the horizontal Pipe *or* stay here and wait for the next Pipe. They both spirit you equal distances ahead; the second Pipe actually carries you past more troubling foes and is worth waiting for. If you didn't take the first Pipe, get a power-up from the ? ahead and beware the next set of overhead Spikes: the darker ones fall when you pass. If you took the first Pipe, you'll emerge before a region with one Ball 'N' Chain on the bottom and four on top. The upper route has Coins; if you can fly up there, it's worth the trip. The ? along the bottom route has a power-up. (Get it and double back, if you want.) If you took the second Pipe, you'll drop out just ahead: if you hit the Dry Bones there over and over, you'll be able to collect as many 1-Ups as you want. Ditto getting under the Block at the end, near the door, and stomping that Dry Bones over and over. When you go through the door, you'll face a wheel of Reznors: get under the perch of each fire-blowing Triceratops and bop it into eternity. It's a cinch!

Cheese Bridge: Time to ride the Pulley Ledges again. There are three levels: go from low to middle to top as the Chainsaws approach, then *stay* on the top, leaping the Chainsaws. Not only is this the safest route, you'll be able to get the ? power-up *and* break the Tape at the end. The ? at the Log Bridge has Yoshi's Wings. Take them and fly into the skies, where Coins and Fuzzies await. If the Wings are no help to you, grab the Rope and ride it ahead, jumping down onto the first Log Bridge. Go right, to the next Rope. *Don't* go into the Pipe ahead: it's a short ride through Bullet Bill territory, one Bill coming at you from each corner simultaneously as you cross moving Ledges. There isn't a single power-up or Coin to gain here. So—back on the Log Bridges, continue heading right: skip the second Rope, but hop from the Pipe to the Log Bridge ahead, then jump down to the next Bridge. Walk ahead or ride the Ropes, depending on your personal preference: when you pass the Pipe and get on the next Rope, climb high and low with care to get past the Chainsaws. If you have Yoshi, do the following at the end: fly Yoshi *below* the top of the Plateau—with the Uprights. As Yoshi's about to drop off the bottom, spin-jump Mario off the dinosaur and land on the Plateau. Walk ahead to—

Soda Lake: This scroll-ahead-by-itself level is the supreme test of your swimming skills, as you head right past Torpedo Teds and Cheep Cheeps. Only sharp eyes and fingers will get you through *most* of this level, but when you reach the second group of three Torpedo Teds in a row—a diagonal line of them, going from upper left to bottom right—you're near the end. At this troublesome trio, swim down and *under* the Plateau on the bottom of the screen, pressing the B button even though you can't see Mario. The Teds won't be able to hurt you.

Butter Bridge 1: This screen scrolls right, so you can't dawdle. The Plateaus ahead sink as you stand on them, so keep hopping until new ones scroll on. The Ledges sink too, so you'll have to leap on them as well. Up ahead you'll be sorry if you don't have a Cape and didn't go to the Red Switch Palace: the red

Blocks ahead *won't* be ahead, and you're going to have a problem getting across. The Plateaus will become increasingly taller and then, suddenly, there won't appear to be any more. Don't fear! Ride the last one down and it will bring low Plateaus into view. Get on the Log Bridge and ride the screen up; naturally, you'll have to spin the rotating Blocks to get through them. Two tall Plateaus, a sinking Ledge, and a Log Bridge . . . and then you're home free!

Cookie Mountain: A beastly little place . . . literally. A Koopa and two Monty Moles welcome you here. Leap the Pit and get under the Blocks ahead; jump up to knock the Sumo Brother off. If you want, go back to the left and climb the Slope: you can Y/A jump even a normal Mario to the top of the ? Blocks ahead if you start running in the V of the Slope. Collect the power-up there, then take care of the Monty below and collect the Coins from the ?'s. Three Koopas attack as you pass the Slopes to the right; you can skip them all or bop them. Climb the Slope to the Plateau: wait until the *two* Monty Moles appear on top before you go after them. Get the Moles on the bottom all together by walking off the Ledge above them, or pick them off one at a time, then continue right. Montys erupt from the Plateau ahead: stop and go past them or bop them. Go past the Pipe: there are two Sumo Brothers on the Note Blocks ahead. And Monty jumps from the ground to add to your troubles under there. Your best bet is to leap onto the Notes and vault from there into the Clouds above—you'll be rewarded with a surprise 1-Up! If you can't get up there, run past the Sumos when they're not flaming. The Pipe beyond has a Pumpkin Piranha.

After you break the Tape, five Montys erupt from the face of the Plateau. Your best bet is to scroll the screen slowly, exposing one at a time and bashing it.

When all four are gone, hit the third Block from the left up ahead to uncover a Vine, climb, jump to the top of the Plateau on the left—leaping from a point somewhat short of the Block above, so you don't hit it when you jump and fall back down—and hit the Block there for a 1-Up. Go back down, enter the Pipe, and swim left. (If you don't want the Coins or a hassle with Porcupuffers, skip the Pipe.) A Monty erupts from the ground beyond, Yoshi can be found in the ? between the two Note Blocks, and another Monty sprouts just beyond. Montys pop from the walls ahead; nothing troublesome here. After the Pipes and Bridges, there are two parallel rows of ?'s, a Sumo Brother on each. Bop off the bottom one, hop up, then get the top one—whose fire burns on the lower row, *not* on the ground. The third ? from the left, on the bottom, contains a power-up; all the rest are Coins. There's a familiar, vicious athlete waiting right before the end; the Block to his right is a single Coin.

Butter Bridge 2: Super Koopas and regular Shell-free Koopas abound: hit the first Super Koopa to get its Cape and soar ahead. Fly into the Clouds for Coins; failing this, simply cross the Log Bridges. Farther on, Koopas will be throwing Shells at you; if you press the right button, you'll cause them to toss before they're ready. After the Tape, you'll pass a Pipe; the next Pipe will take you to a Coin zone where you do your Rope-hanging trick. Exit and continue right; no surprises.

Ludwig's Castle: Stomp the Bony Beetle when its Spike is withdrawn—or, if you have a Cape, you can whip them—then make your way past the lone Ball 'N' Chain, climbing to the Block above it and then to the top of the wall on the right. Wait for the next Beetle to wander your way, then drop on it, head to the next Ball 'N' Chain, and get set to stop and go through a tunnel filled with Ball 'N' Chains. The *only* way you're going to get through here is by crouching in the lower right corner after passing the first Ball 'N' Chain on the bottom of the upper tunnel, then crouching over the hub of the next Ball 'N' Chain on the bottom. It helps if you're normal-sized Mario here. A power-up and door await you after this. However, you may want to try something else. After you pass the last of the Ball 'N' Chains, *stop*. See the single Block overhead, the one that's part of the ceiling? You can jump right through it! Do so, head right, and—if you've got a Cape—fly up to a Pipe! Inside is a bonus room that will let you out the same place as the door.

The Spiked ceiling's closing in on you in the next section: hurry ahead, watching out for the Lava Pits and Lava Bubbles. Hit the On/Off Switch ahead: that will cause the ceiling to go back up where it belongs. Continue left and exit. The next room is a vertical climb up and to the right for a power-up, then back to the left. Just beware the Spikes and Koopas here as you pick your way to the top. Enter the door and continue right. When Ludwig appears, leap the fireballs and jump onto his head. He'll crawl into his Shell and scoot at you; leap the Shell until he comes out, then jump the fireballs and hit him again. It's possible to get in two knocks at once; in any case, three raps in all and he's history.

Forest of Illusion

Forest of Illusion 1: After knocking some sense into the Wiggler's head and taking care of the Koopa on the other side of the Pit, get a power-up from the ? on the right. Hop right with care, as there are Koopas on the Plateaus ahead: hop on each noggin twice to decapitate the creatures *and* send their Koopa bodies off the cliff. Or you can save a head and use it on: another

Wiggler ahead. The ? above is Yoshi. Use the Jumping Board ahead to enable Yoshi to eat the Fruit; go back and eat a Fruit you already passed. A Cloud will arrive, dropping bonus Faces! Get a 1-Up from the Block amidst the Note Blocks ahead. Get it by hitting a Note Block to make it hop out or by going right and jumping left, onto the Blocks. A rash of Wigglers will greet you when you head right again, but they're easily clobbered. You'll find a power-up Block ahead: pick a Super Star and charge forward, earning 1-Ups as you mow enemies down. (If you kill yourself here —which is highly recommended—you can go back and repeat: you'll be able to collect an unlimited number of 1-Ups this way!) If you didn't get the Super Star, be very careful: those Blocks up ahead contain Koopas and Goombas. If you did get the Super Star, you should run out of steam when the Koopa and Wiggler are crawling ahead of you in a dip in the Logs: use the head of the former to dismantle the latter, but stay out of the depression or you'll get mowed down too. Stop the head by jumping on it—or just hop over it—then drop down to the Ledge at the end. Get a P Balloon from it and float left to get the Key from the Block there. (The Balloon is easier caught while jumping the Pit to the right; jumping up at the Block is tough.) The Key will allow you to enter the Blue Switch Palace. If you didn't get in—continue right, look out for the Hammer Brother beyond the Pipe, and continue to the end, which is near.

Forest of Illusion 2: Great: more swimming. Cheep Cheeps prowl, and Urchins rise and fall: avoid the former and watch the patterns of the latter to make your way through. The first ! gives you a Cape. Go ahead, past the two Urchins—wait until one is up or down, go past, then wait for the other to rise—drop down and rush up to beat the school of Cheep Cheeps coming from the right, rise up past the Urchin and get the Dragon Coin, wait to the right of the blue Block on the right for the Urchin ahead to go down, then swim up, right, and down around the Urchin Block to the left, continue to drop left, and go right on the bottom before the school of Cheep Cheeps passes—they're coming from the left. Swim up, weaving between the Cheep Cheeps. Get a power-up from the ? on top. Drop straight down to the bottom, go right, and swim up to the chamber to the left of Rip Van Fish. There are four invisible Blocks there. Hit up under the right two first: the leftmost of those two has a 1-Up. Let it drift to the left and fall out. Catch it, *then* hit the other two invisible Blocks. (Obviously, if you hit the two Blocks on the left first, the 1-Up will be trapped in there!) Go left, up, and right at the first opening. Wait until the two Urchins rise, go under them, continue ahead, and stay on the top. You'll find another Dragon Coin; continue right. Drop down when you can, get a power-up from the ! on the bottom, and swim *left* along the bottom, right over the Rip Van Fish. The wall isn't real, and the Blue Switch Palace Key is on the other side. Inside, take the two P's and put them on the right side of the room. Get on the Pipe, nab the two Coins on the right, hit the Switches, and go to it!

Forest of Illusion 3: Bubbles—rotten Bubbles carrying Bob-Ombs and Goombas! When you reach the Jumping Board, go over the Pipe, get Yoshi from the ?, and enter the Pipe to the right. You should end up with at least two 1-Ups in this easy bonus room. Get Coins from the second of the diagonal Blocks ahead and leap the Pit. When you reach the two Blocks, hit the lower Block so the head will bash the upper Block and dislodge the Jumping Board. Carry the Jumping Board to the tall Pipe ahead and vault over it. Bop your Bubble-borne foes and break the Tape ahead; watch for the Bubble with the power-up that comes floating along after two Goomba Bubbles. Cross the Pipes and continue right. When you reach the ?'s ahead, all have Coins; so do all the ?'s leading to the next Pipe. A multiplying Chargin' Chuck waits beyond; bop or avoid the fiend and the other foes raining from the Bubble-filled skies, tap the Blocks then leap on them to clear the Pipe, and exit.

Forest Ghost House: Y-button rush to the right, luring Big Blue Boo and attendants in that direction; when you come to the depression in the floor, crouch in the left corner. The Eerie coming from the right will pass right overhead. Continue racing ahead; lure the next Big Blue to the left by jumping up and down in its chamber; duck under it and go ahead at a walk. (If you run, there'll be two ghosts by the steps you have to jump instead of one.) After you leap up the steps with the specter perched on it, *then* you can Y-button through the rest of the hallway. When you clear it, fly if you have a Cape. If not, race ahead to the door, watching out for Eeries. The first ? you encounter en route will have a Coin, the second ? a power-up. Next room: Y-button race ahead of the ghosts. Go under the Blocks ahead and get a 1-Up from the golden Block. Turn back and go up, but don't hit the P Switch: if you do, it'll seal up the Coins and make it impossible for you to reach the doors below. Don't enter the first door at the end: you'll find yourself back at the end of the hallway. The second door will take you to the top of the Ghost House and access to the doors there. Go left: the first door will take you to the end; the second door will take you to the end *and* a 3-Up Moon!

Forest of Illusion 4: If you didn't go to the Ghost

House, you'll enter the Forest of Illusion 4 halfway through. If you did visit the Ghost House, throw a Shell at the Fishin' Lakitu and appropriate its Cloud for the trip right. When you reach the Pipe, you can get a full supply of 1-Ups: throw a Shell between the Pipe and the rim of the depression—on the left. When the Fishin' Lakitu throws Spinies into that stretch of land, the ricocheting Shell will supply you with unlimited 1-Ups. When you reach the Tape—which is where the Ghost Houseless players have been waiting —bop the Lakitu in a Pipe, cross the Pit, and—if you can Fly—bop the Lakitu in a Pipe and go down. If you can't, hit the P Switch and collect the Coins. On the steps, crouch on the top one to avoid the Koopa bopping your way from the right. The middle Pipe of the three green ones ahead leads to a Coin-filled water realm; swim left and, when you exit, you'll be back at the Tape. Back at the green Pipes, cross between the Spiny rain and hit the ? on top of the Blocks ahead for a power-up. The ?'s on the other side give you Coins. Take a head with you: when you reach the pyramids of blue Blocks ahead, the Fishin' Lakitu will give you unlimited 1-Ups as before. Just stay out of the way. Chargin' Chuck's at the end, so be ready for him!

Forest Secret Area: Fly ahead if you can; the alternative is to ride the Ledges. The only place with anything new is the end: if both Ledges are on the screen when you cross through the Uprights *without* hitting the Tape, you'll earn a passel o' points and a 1-Up.

Forest Fortress: Crushing Columns await in the scrolling section; you've had experience with these and they shouldn't present a problem. Grinders can be passed without difficulty—well, without *much* difficulty, anyway—by watching them and timing your moves and, wherever possible, using Blocks to cross (in the second section). You can't destroy the Grinders, but you can spin jump off of them. In the second section, pass under the inverted L-shaped Ledge overhead at the beginning and press L and R: the Grinders here will vanish. After crossing on the overhead Blocks beyond, press R and the Grinder will drop off the Ledge so you can pass. If you have a Cape, don't enter the door at the end here but go up over the Ledge above it and continue right. Fly over the Lava and collect the nine 1-Ups in Blocks before the door. In any case, both doors lead to Renzor. Fight as you did before and move on to—

Roy's Castle: You're going to be seeing more of these things later: snaking Ledges that crawl along. You can't just stand on them or they'll creep out from under you; when they make stairs, you've got to climb. The set at the bottom of the narrow tunnel is pretty easy: just remember that when the front drops and starts back the way it came, under your section, *stand still*: when the section you're on vanishes, you'll fall on solid Ledge. The Lava Bubbles here are easy to avoid. Don't get off when the "snake" enters the Spike zone . . . but do watch out for falling Spikes. You can tell by their discoloration the ones that are gonna drop. When you enter the second chamber, get off and climb down the steps. Grab the P Switch under the Spikes and carry it to the right of the Statue of Bowser. Hit L then touch the P for a 1-Up. Roy's chamber is up ahead. He does the same thing as Morton, but the room is slightly different: the walls move in slowly! You aren't going to have as much time to finish Roy off.

Chocolate Island

Chocolate Island 1: Dino Rhino welcomes you to this new land: crush the monster and it becomes Mini

Dino, shooting flame from its mouth. In other words, don't stomp it again right away! Another two Minis roll in from the Slopes ahead. When you get on top of the Plateau, a power-up will pop from the bushes and a flying ? will bring you another. Cross over the first Pipe but get into the second: it'll Cannon you ahead. Use the Jumping Board to cross the Tape. Up ahead: a P Switch and Munchers. Use the trusty P to solidify the Coins, but be prepared to fight Chargin' Chuck. After the twin Slopes, fly up to the Clouds if you can. If not, continue ahead, stomping all the prehistoric pests, collecting the power-up from the flying ?, and getting a good Y-button start so you can clear the Pit ahead. Get Yoshi from the ? beyond, a power-up from the ! over the row of !'s, and then get outta there by crawling into the little gray Pipe after the third blue one. It'll Cannon you to the end.

Choco-Ghost House: The floor's got holes that move back and forth, and there are usually Eeries flying above them when you try to jump. (Funny how that works out!) If you've got a Cape, great. If not—you'll have your hands full. Don't hesitate to backtrack whenever necessary. Start out by Y-buttoning ahead without stopping. You'll clear the hole, the first two Eeries; leap to the Ledge, leap down—still at top speed—and leap over the flock of Eeries. Slow down then, because things are always different hereafter. There are more holes, more Eeries, then a Fishin' Boo just ahead. Don't be intimidated by the rod-packing spook: if you walk—*never* jump—its burnin' line won't touch you. Of course, that may be a problem with Eeries coming from the left and right, but at least don't jump when the line is *near* you. When you reach the door, don't try to enter unless there's a floor beneath it. Next section: Boo-Blocks attack. They come at you when you look at them; they turn back to

Blocks when you look away. Sucker them into plays
where you need to do some climbing! The door is up
above.

Chocolate Island 2: Use the Jumping Board: there's an
invisible Block below and to the right of the Coin
above. The ? at the top is Yoshi, but be careful: the
Mini-Dino's flame can reach you even if you're
perched "safely" atop the Block. Enter the Pipe at the
bottom right. Ahead: Slopes. Lots of them, with
Koopas and other fiends on patrol. This is an unusual
area in that there are Coins and power-ups ahead, and
plenty of foes . . . but no strategy, per se. If you
can't walk the Slopes—which slant both ways—and
you aren't flying, you won't make it through here.

Chocolate Island 3: A series of rotating Ledges will
lead you through the early part of this section; though
there are Koopas on the hubs, they won't bother you
if you don't bother them. If you're having trouble getting to the third rotating Ledge of the three in a row,
all you have to do is note that the second and third
are rotating at the same time and match when yours is
at three o'clock and the other is at nine. Move to the
left side of your Ledge and Y-jump ahead, timing the
jump so you and the Ledge will intersect! Get the
power-up from the ? below to the right, and when
you reach the downward-facing Pipe, go up. You'll
find yourself in a land of one moving Ledge and one
rotating one. When you've swept up enough Coins to
satisfy King Midas, leap off the rotating Ledge to the
right and go down the Pipe—which is out of sight
below; but don't worry, you'll make it. When you
emerge, you'll be well along this realm. If you didn't
get in, then you've crossed more Ledges like the one
from before. Hereafter, Fuzzies dog your trail: knee

and you'll be okay. If you can't fly, hit the Block at the end to reach the Uprights.

Chocolate Fortress: You've got to make your way through pencillike Spikes: they come in pairs at the start, one upper, one lower, and close together. Obviously you don't want to get pinched between them! You don't even want to get nicked, or you die. Dry Bones make the leaping difficult. After the bubbling Pit—covered with red ! if you went to the Red Switching Palace—go under the Spike ahead and, when it's starting on its way up, race ahead and jump: it operates in tandem with a Spike that's just out of view. But if the one behind you was starting up, so was the one in front. There's a Dry Bones waiting on the other side of this Pit, so try to land on the left side of the Ledge and leap *at once* to the ? above it. Not only will you have to bop the Bones, but there are flames shooting at you from the right. Hit the Dry Bones, get a power-up from the ?, and leap to the right when the Spike ahead is gone and there are no fireballs. Piece of cake! There's another Pit ahead and, after it, a Spike *rising* from the ground. With fireballs still acomin'. And a Spike coming down on the other side of the next Pit. Timing and patience are the keys here.

After you get through this mess, there are more Spikes, Thwimps and Thwomps. Nothing new; even Reznor's a rehash when you get to the end.

Chocolate Island 4: It's safe to slide down the Slope. When you get to the bottom, an odd sort of Ledge will appear; being one never to look a gift lift in the mouth, take it! Ride it up, scoot down the Slope to the Ledge on the bottom—ignoring the two Ledges to your right—ride the one below up to the Dragon Coin. Go up and over the Slope, jump to the Ledge below, then get off that one for the one that appears

underneath. Go from *that* one to the one above/right
which is parallel to it—not the one above that, facing
the upper right. Leap from this one to the Ledge coming at it—*this* one is facing the upper right. Leap from
that to the Ledge on the bottom. Get on and off it fast
'cause it'll sink; go up the Slope, down the side, and
into the area with the three 1-Ups and a power-up—
you don't need the Ledges here. If you haven't done
any blue switching, you won't be able to reach this
region without the Ledges. When you've got everything, take the last Ledge on the right and ride it up.
You'll come to a series of Blocks. There's a diagonal
row of gold Blocks running from upper left to lower
right. Hit the third one from the top to expose a P
Switch. Activate it and drop down the chute *below* the
one with the Dragon Coin. Enter the Pipe. Activate
the P Switch here and just fall, collecting Coins—and
watching the right side for any power-ups you want.
Eventually, the Coins will become Blocks and you'll
have to exit. The ? to the right of the Pipe has a
power-up. Jump down and keep an eye out for—how
could you miss it?—Mega Mole: hop on its back for a
ride across the Lava ahead. (Jump carefully: you can
miss and the Mole will kill you!) If another Mole
bumps it, your Mole will change direction. So be prepared to switch mounts if need be.

Chocolate Island 5: Go up into the first square of gold
Blocks and get Yoshi. Pick up the P Switch and move
it—otherwise, you'll fall to your death when the
Blocks beneath it become Coins. Activate it and enter
the Pipe. You'll usually come away from the bonus
room with three 1-Ups. You'll also be just a hop, skip
and jump (literally) from the midpoint of the level.
Cross the Pipes, but don't be fooled by the accordion
Ledge ahead; it extends horizontally and *then* vertically. Ditto the two after it. Fortunately, they do it in

tandem, so you can cross, wait on the middle block, and cross again. There's a Chargin' Chuck on the second Pipe over and three on the Plateau right after. Good idea to go back and get a Koopa head from a nearby Ledge to "chuck" at the latter bunch! (If you're not powered-up here, go left, cross two "ponds," and enter the Pipe. Go right: Mushrooms will float your way in the Bubbles. Catch one as you head right, enter the Pipe, and you'll be right back here.)

Chocolate Secret: Chocolate Island 2 got you here: here's how to get out! After Blargg comes and goes, hit the Jumping Board to reach the other side of the Lava. The foes up ahead are Chargin' Chucks and Buzzy Beetles. After you pass through the narrow tunnel, do the following if you can fly: kill all the Buzzy Beetles except one. When it's in the area between the Chucks, spin it until it flies up and hits the Footballs for points and 1-Ups. *Don't* go up the downward-facing green Pipe: lots of pain with Hammer Brothers and others, and no gain. Enter the Pipe at the end and ski down the Slopes: if you keep your pad pressed down, you'll mow the Buzzy Beetles down. The ones on the bottom are easily squashed. Cross the last region with quick jumps on the Columns: they'll be sinking into the Lava! Where there are Slopes here, use them to your advantage to slide against foes; some, like Chucks, may take two or three attacks.

Wendy's Castle: When you enter here, Y-button ahead, leap the Dry Bones, use the Jumping Board *on its right side*, and get up to the right before the thorny Spike comes crashing down. (You *can* stand in the lower right corner rather than jump immediately, but only if you bopped Dry Bones as you rushed by.) When you get up to the Plateau and hurry right, drop down—assuming ol' Dry didn't throw a Bone, which *will* continue this far right—and rush ahead: get into the niche ahead before the Grinder comes by to mash you. Rush ahead when it's passed and leap *up* into the space overhead when the two Grinders come crashing at you. If you can't land betwixt them, a spin jump will keep you from being pulverized. Follow the rightward-rolling Grinder and wait at the Lava Pit for the Lava Bubble to pass before you jump to the Block ahead—there will be two red Blocks for easier jumping if you did the switcheroo earlier. Jump off to the right when the Lava Bubble falls away, and watch the patterns of the Grinders and big Spikes ahead so that you can make your way through here.

The second half of the Castle is populated with Li'l Sparkies and Hotheads; if you can't get past one with a jump, use a spin-jump. It'll live, but at least you won't die. When you come to the ceilings that are coming to you—coming down, that is—race ahead and you'll be okay. Wendy's red door is ahead: like Lemmy, there's one real Koopa and two bogus ones. If you need to recuperate at any point, straddle the second and third Pipes from the left; attacks there are comparatively light.

Sunken Ghost Ship: Put your trunks back on and take a dip! Cannons are firing at you as you make your way through the submerged wreck. After getting the power-up, swim up and right: when you reach the wall of Blocks just beyond the Crate, hover there. Knock down the Mini-Ninja's as they're fired your way from either the top or bottom Cannon. You'll earn points, then 1-Ups. Hit to your heart's content—it doesn't matter if you run out of time: just start again!—then drop down the gold Pipe in the bottom right. The next room is full of Eeries and Disappearing Boo Buddys—this is a *ghost* ship, remember, so stay put when they vanish, because they'll reappear in some other configuration. (Or you can cheat: hold down/right on the pad and jab B continuously. *Most* of the time, you'll sail right through the ghosts.) When you reach the end and fall in the vertical room, grab Super Stars to beat your flying foes; land on the Ledge and get another as you drop. When you pass through the break in the floor, skew toward the right and grab the Crystal below.

Valley of Bowser

Valley of Bowser 1: If you hit the Red Switch Palace, the Mega Mole in here will be sealed up. If not, you'll have to get past the brute *and* the Chargin' Chuck beyond. Take the middle level to the right, wait for the Mole to fall in the depression, and continue right. Leap the one who comes down the stairs, climb the stairs, go down the other side, and *don't* drop off into the water. You don't want to go near where the Chucks are pounding through the Blocks below. Jump up to the Ledge above that, pass under the triangular excavation in the ceiling, continue right, and break the Tape. Go left and onto the Ledge above this: ride Mega Mole across the Munchers. Go down, left on the first Ledge you come to, and right: drop down at the end and go left to hit the ! for a power-up. (Assuming you visited the Green Switch Palace . . .) Go to the ! Blocks ahead and get them—if you can fly—then continue right. Go right along the bottom tunnel; spin-jump the Mole that dares to get in your way. Continue right and do the same to the two Chucks—or heave the blue Blocks at them. Enter the Pipe and you're through.

Valley of Bowser 2: Columns are rising up while Swoopers and Koopas attack; nothing too challenging here, though. The first ? has a power-up—watch for the head that comes rolling from the right just as you get here—so does the ! at the end. (You don't really want it, though: normal Mario is best suited to get through the area that follows.) There are nothing but Coins in between. Clearly, you've got to watch out for loose heads in here: they'll bounce between the high walls, clobbering you if you're in the middle. Next section: the ? will give you Yoshi Wings, which you can fly straight up for a skyload of Coins. Back on the ground, continue right as the floor and ceiling rise and fall. Wait till everything is starting on its way up before you enter: you'll pick out the patterns very quickly—niches in the floor and ceiling are the places you want to be—but for impatient types, here's how to go through:

Get in the opening facing you when it's level with the floor. Walk under the horizontal Ledge ahead and over the vertical one beyond it and keep going over the small Ledge beyond; stop at the outcropping at the top and ride the wall all the way down . . . even if you don't want the Coins on the right. Go up with the wall when it rises and plant yourself in the niche on top. Run ahead and go down at the vertical Ledge. Go and get the Dragon Coin if you want it, then come back and go under the vertical Ledge. Ride the wall up, and when it's on the way back down, run ahead to the niche in the floor. When the floor rises, run ahead to the inverted T-shaped Ledge ahead and cross over the top to the outcropping on top—you can go left here for the Dragon Coin if you want to risk it. When the wall comes down, run ahead to the long niche on the bottom, directly ahead. Cross, next, to the niche on top and plant yourself on the left side. Don't go down here: the corridor on the bottom right is a dead end. When the wall goes down, ride it: when it goes up, head to the next niche on top. When it goes down, scoot down the stairs, to the bottom, and wait

164

to the left of the vertical Ledge overhead. Ride the wall up again, into the niche above. When the wall comes down, go over that vertical Ledge, down, and right at the bottom. Stop when you're directly under a vertical opening with a small niche on top and a large one to the right. Just stay put! When the wall comes down again, amble to the right and wait at the bottom, your nose pressed to the outcropping: when the wall rises, run like mad along the bottom to the next vertical passageway and, without stopping for breath or to sightsee, run right and out the Pipe or go down for the Coins if you have the time . . . and courage. There, that was easy.

The floor's rising when you get to the next room so dash ahead pronto, up the stairs, or you'll be crushed —the Pipe niche is not a safe place. Make sure you run right to the lip of the cliff, or the rising wall will get you. There's a Mega Mole below you, but don't worry about that bully yet; get on top of the golden wall that was rising just seconds before. Leap up (yes, up), right off the screen. Go left: you'll go past the steps, past the Pipe, and you'll drop into a screen with a Key. Pick it up and put it in the hole: that will let you into—

Valley Fortress: Biiiig Spikes again. They lower a bit before they fall: wait until they've risen, then run past the first three, hit the ! if it's there, run past the next four in one gulp, and leap onto the Ledge over the golden Spike pit. You'll be standing *under* golden Spikes as well; don't move until you've pressed the R button to scroll the screen and shake loose the falling golden Spikes before you get to them. Don't stay put too long, though: Dry Bones will be coming along, hurling Bones, and you don't want to be under Spikes when you jump them. There's a Bony Beetle and a second Dry Bones as well. When you cross that troublesome area, cross under one big Spike, then another; when you come to the next three, take all three Ledges quickly, without stopping, or you won't clear them. In the next room are more Spikes, falling faster than ever. When your careful timing gets you to the other side, you'll face the final Reznor. Beat as before. It's important to win here: when you do, a path will open up to the ninth chamber of Bowser's Castle (see below: it starts with the ? you have to hit for light). What's more, if you come at it this way, there'll be a Tape for you to break at the end, which will enable you to get right back to Bowser if he kills you—which he will, often. The Tape and Uprights don't show up if you take the *normal* route.

Valley Ghost House: Bubble alert! Get the power-up above, continue right when the Bubble disappears, jump down the steps over the next one, leap to the Ledge—the Bubble will miss you—and stop on the lowest Ledge until the Bubble appears: leap over it and race ahead to the door. You'll find yourself on a ledge with a P Switch above. Hit the Block to dislodge it, activate it and *race* to the right. If a Super Star falls, don't stop to collect it unless it falls right next to you on the right: nothing will save you if you don't clear the Ledge before the P power wears out! Leap ahead, using Y-button power, jumping Eeries and Pits—two huge Y-button jumps, when jumps are needed, will get you across everything; when you reach permanently solid ground, don't slow down: the Coins here will solidify when the P wears out! You'll pass several doors: run to the one on the end, get the 1-Up there—in addition to the 1-Up you got from all the Coins you collected under here if you were Super Mario—and enter. You'll find a P Switch, but you don't want to hit it here. Carry it to the right—over the Blocks and up through the fake floor above when you seem to be trapped—put it down immediately to the right of the solo Block you find here, hit the Block, and place yourself smack against the left side of the P Switch. A stream of Coins will extend from the Block; you will be using your control pad to create a stairway of Coins up and right. The reason you're leaning against the Switch is twofold: first, by not moving, you prevent any of the Boos from moving; and second, you don't want to inadvertently let yourself out the door to the right. Moving your pad up while you're in front of it will do that. When the music stops, hit the Switch, climb the stairs, and get into the room in the upper right; your Blocks had better be flush with the door, because you've got to squat to be able to fit. If you step up three, over three, up three, etc., you should have no trouble. Use the Key to unlock the Castle. (If you messed up, you won't get a second chance; though you can go to the door on the right and go back to the room with the first P Switch, the all-important Coin Block will only give you one measly Coin when you return to it.)

Valley of Bowser 3: Three hoppin' Koopas greet you; when you get past them, you'll find a power-up in the ?. The Elevators here are numbered: the shortest are one, the longest are four. Get off them before they hit zero, when they disappear. You can walk on the Cables, however, so it isn't imperative that you ride the first ones (no pun intended). The third will take you to a series of ones that will get you across the next area to the white Column. Go from the one to the next one, then onto the Pipe. Go down the bottom Pipe. You'll usually get two 1-Ups in this bonus room. When you exit, hit the Jumping Board to break the Tape, then move it to the right of the ? to get the power-up. Use the Board once again to get to the top Ledge on the right—though if you miss it, you can hop up from the others. Koopas haunt the diagonal Cables here. Ride the Ledges across and you'll reach the end of the level. It will be necessary to hop on the backs of the Banzai Bills here to get across.

Valley of Bowser 4: The Chuck ahead is shoveling Rocks that look like Soccer balls this time. Rush down the Slope after the first one passes. If you're normal Mario, the only way you're going to get here—unless you can kill Chuck and leap from his perch—is to jump off the head of the Koopa that comes from the right, land on the sinking Ledge in the Lava, and Y-button off it before it goes under. Go up the Slope quickly, hopping the one Rock and bashing Chuck before he can shovel out more. Hit the ! for a power-up; when Chuck follows you down, jump on the Block then over to the Pipe. Stand on the right edge: Chuck will self-destruct when he leaps up against your feet. Cross the Lava with quick leaps from the three floating Ledges—you can Y-button across or take it more slowly, using the heads of the Koopas there for boosts—and enter the Pipe beyond *if* you want to go through an ice realm with a few power-ups *and* end up back on the left side of the three Lava Ledges! In any event, beyond the Lava—and the entrance Pipe—is a Block: hit it to release a Vine. You'll find Yoshi in the ? at the top. Go right and drill down the golden Blocks, skewing right: you want to land on the first Ledge you see, not the one floating in the Lava below. The Block at the end has a 1-Up that will roll to the right. Drop down off the right side of the Ledge, hit the Lava Ledges, and be there to catch it. Simple! On the other side, though, more Rocks come rollin' from Chuck. After him, there's one Lava Ledge and then the Tape. On the other side: another Rockin' Chuck. Jump the first Rock—standing with your face pressed to the wall—race ahead before another is thrown and hit Chuck on the head, vault to the ! Block (Chuck'll probably follow you and perish in the Lava) and get the power-up from the ? above; then Y-button across the Lava Ledge, past the next rolling-stone Chuck, climb the Plateau—after first going to the lower right corner so the screen will scroll correctly up ahead—and drop down onto the Lava Ledge . . . when Rocks aren't falling onto it! (You wouldn't see the Ledge if you hadn't hit the corner of the Plateau!) Go down the Slope beyond, onto the Lava Ledge, past the Chuck, and so on to the end of the level.

Larry's Castle: Ball 'N' Chains. Are you sick of 'em? Hope not, because they welcome you here. Along with a long Ledge you've met before, back in Roy's Castle: the one that moves around like a snake. But the ride isn't going to be as easy this time. When the round begins, you'll be on a Ledge that's crawling forward. Walk ahead with it—and up, when it forms little steps—all the while leaping or holding back to avoid the Ball 'N' Chains. When you pass under the lower solid Block over the Lava, leap onto it. Then, when the "snake" heads up, leap on its top Block—its head, if you will. Ride it up just a bit. It'll turn left; when it does, stand directly over the solid Block below . . . that is, the Block to the upper left of the previous Block you were standing on. When the Ledge crawls away, you'll drop down onto that upper left Block. Now . . . just stand there. The snaking Ledge will pass overhead at 225 on the timer; watch it go by, but stay put. At 214 on the timer the Ledge will appear on your right. Jump up to it at once—Y-button for added lift—it won't be coming back. The Ledge is going to crawl back and forth now, under itself; keep dropping down onto it, avoiding the Ball 'N' Chain down there, and stay with the Ledge as it forms steps and goes up the right. Enter the door at the end. There are doors at the top and bottom; though they both lead to the same place, the one on the bottom lets you break the Tape *and* gives you a power-up. Obviously you want that one, so that if you die, you won't have to go crawling around again! Get to it by standing on any Block of the Ledge: they'll all fold into the downward-moving Ledge and, instead of getting off, you can ride it down the Pit that's in front of the upper door. (If you can fly, it's possible to avoid the Ledges altogether as you make your way through Ball 'N' Chain land.)

Pretty standard fare up ahead: you'll slide down a little Escalator, come to a Dry Bones or two, and wait in the right-hand corner while a Magikoopa appears and flings some magic. The wizard will appear at the left edge of the Plateau above, then the right; go up after the Magikoopa vanishes from the right. Reason? Next stop is directly to your left. Just make sure you don't run into the two Pencil Spikes above in your haste to get away! Don't tarry either, though: next stop is the right side of the Plateau again. Go past the pair of pencil-like Spikes—take them both in one dash. When you come to the wall, a Magikoopa will bust holes in it for you—unless you're Caped, in which case you can do it yourself. Just make sure the magic doesn't fry you as well. There's a narrow Lava Pit on the other side, another set of Spikes with a Magikoopa in front—or above or to your left, depending on the sorcerer's mood—and a Koopa wandering around, freed by magic from the wall . . . all at once! There's also a ! above with a power-up. Another Dry Bones and Lava Pit await, another wall of Blocks that only a Cape or magic can bust, and two sets of Spikes behind it, each closing in on one another like teeth. A larger Lava Pit is after that. All the Lava Pits, incidentally, spit Lava Bubbles, just to make things exciting. Magikoopa will also be waiting there.

When you finally meet Larry—which is very soon hereafter—you'll find him identical to Iggy, with one exception: balls of Lava shoot up at you. There's no destroying these; you have to rush to the opposite side whenever they sizzle your way.

Front Door: You've made it to the Castle. You'll find four doors in the hallway; each puts you through a different kind of challenge, and all lead to the same place. The first has crushing Columns, a screen that scrolls, and fireballs shooting up at you. The second's got a wire Fence to cross like you did way back in Iggy's Castle—though now there are Lava Bubbles swooping at you in addition to Koopas—and it's the easiest to get through. Just stay on the Fence, crawling along the bottom.

All four doors have led you to the fifth through ninth. Five are those big thorny Spikes and Thwomps coming down at you—easiest: stand right up against the first Spike and when it rises, run through nonstop with the Y-button pressed—six is a swim through Spikes, Ball 'N' Chains, and Dry Bones, with some Dry Fish lending a fin; seven are little Bowsers attacking you and Bowser Statues shooting fire, with Lava Bubbles thrown in for bad measure; and eight is a hallway filled with Football-tossin' Chucks.

Next up: room number nine. Actually, it's a hallway that leads to Bowser. Go right and hit the ? to shed some light on the situation. There's a Mini-Ninja beyond, some Columns in the Lava, a Mini-Ninja and Mechakoopas after that, and so on; they won't present much of a problem. (In fact, you can wait for the Mechakoopa to come forward, then just leap it, run under the Mini-Ninja, and get set for the next bunch o' Ninjas! Failing this, spin-jump the Mechakoopa to eternity.)

When you get through, it's time to fight the guy who's name is up in lights at the front of the Castle: Bowser. He begins his assault by swooping over you, left and right, tossing Mechakoopas now and then. Spin-jump to knock the Mechakoopas out, then throw them at the big guy. Two hits and Bowser will leave; stay on your toes, though, as a rain of flame comes down. All you can do is stay out of the way. When Bowser returns, Princess Toadstool will put in an appearance—nice of her!—to give you a power-up. What Bowser has for you isn't as pleasant: a pair of Bowling Balls. You can't stop these but, once again, you can stun the Mechakoopas and throw them at the boss. For his final run at you, Bowser will hip-hop his clown transport across the ground, trying to grind you in. Once again your only defense is to stay out from under him; your best offense is to fling Mechakoopas back at him.

Succeed, and you win. If not . . . it's back into the fray!

In addition to the regular routes to Bowser, you can warp around through the Star World. You can actually get to the king in very few moves: Yoshi's Island 2, 3, 4, Iggy's Castle, Donut Plains 1, Donut Secret 1, Donut Secret House, Star World 1, 2, 3, 4 . . . and then the Front Door.

Here's how to get through each of the worlds of the Star World:

Star World 1: Smash the Blocks underfoot for bonuses. Make sure you stop and get the Key in the second Block section, on the right side.

Star World 2: Get the special blue Yoshi from the Egg and be able to swim through here at top speeds! Get the Super Star for invincibility and collect another in the ? ahead. Go *under* the Pipe block at the end and swim right for the Key.

Star World 3: Activate the P and collect the Coins dropped by the Lakitu. Pick up a Block and throw it up at the creature, then hop on the Cloud and use it to drift up to the Key—in the ?—and Keyhole. (If you have a Cape, you can forget about the Lakitu.)

Star World 4: Get the red Yoshi from the Egg and let the dinosaur eat Koopas as you carry it across the rotating Ledges: just throw your pal ahead of you if you have to. The first Block has a Cape. This is a longer section than the others, and Koopas are plentiful. You'll find the Key in the ? under the two Pipes at the end. You can hit the ? using a Shell or by flicking it with your Cape.

Star World 5: The Ledges sink, so move across them with haste—though not *so* much haste that the Winged Koopa Troopas pulverize you as you make your way ahead. When you come to the P, *don't* activate it. Take it down to the Plateau, hit the solo Block on the right to release a row of Coins going right, *then* use the P. It'll turn the Coins into a Ledge. (Make sure you're pressing the pad to the right so the Coins head in the proper direction! Keep it pressed until the music stops.) Cross the Ledge to the row of four Blocks ahead, activate the third one from the left into a Vine, and climb. Head right on the path up here. Get the Key at the end. (If you messed up for whatever reason, you can always get the Key by flying up on the left side of the green Pipe at the end. If you can't fly, you can exit and try again!)

When you win this world, enter the Star in the center and you'll head to a realm that has no bearing on the fight against Bowser, but will give you a heckuva lot of training:

Special World

Gnarly: Use the Ledge on the left to spring up; hit the four Blocks to create Vines, and climb up the third from the left. Go up through the gold Block, get the Dragon Coin, and continue up the rightmost Vine. Stop at the point where the Vine passes between two Ledges: the Block on the right continues the Vine, and the Block on the left gives you a P Switch. Bop the Koopa by standing on the right Block and stomping its head, then pick up the P Switch and take it with you. When the Vine ends, use the Note Blocks to spring up to the top set of Blocks. Use the P Switch there and jump down the right side *quickly*: a Block will appear briefly in front of the Pipe one-third of the way down, on the right. That Block is the only way you'll be able to get into the Pipe. If you miss it, don't sweat *too* much. All you'll have missed is a batch of Dragon Coins to the left and a trio of 1-Ups to the right. If you missed the Pipe, drop down from the top, staying to the left; look for a string of Note Blocks and fly to the left of them for a 1-Up. Enter the Pipe at the bottom.

See the P Switches to your left? Pick up one of the blue ones and hit the other two. That'll create a Ledge to your right. Cross, carrying the third P Switch, and use it when the Ledge ends so you can extend it. Watch out for the Amazing Flying Hammer Brother tossing Mallets for all here. (If you want to be daring —and what true Marioite doesn't? —hit all three P's at once, then get under the Hammer Brother and knock him off his perch. Jump onto it and *fly* over to the Plateau on the right.) Exit on the right.

Tubular: Make your way right past the Chargin

Chucks and Jumpin' Piranha Plant until you reach the Pipe with the stack of Blocks to its right. Drop down to the Jumping Board, let if vault you up to the ?, ingest the Power Balloon, hit the P Switch, and collect the oodles of Coins floating in the air. Just make sure the Chargin' Chucks on the right side of the Coin field don't bop you with their Baseballs! (Make sure you do all of this without Yoshi: the poor dinosaur's dead weight in this Tubular zone.)

Beyond them are Volcano Plants and Winged Koopa Troopas, all of whom want a piece of you—so travel with caution. Fly at the top of the screen, dropping only to hit the ? Blocks and knock your enemies into oblivion. Unfortunately, there's no real pattern you can follow, since even an instant's delay in one sector will cause what follows to be different. *Because of the difficulty of maneuvering through this level after the Coin field, Tubular is unquestionably the most challenging region of the game!*

Way Cool: Ridin' the rails—more accurately, the wires —is the theme of this level as you travel via Pulley Ledges. As before, use the "On" and "Off" Blocks to change the direction of the Pulley wires ahead of you —that is, if there are Coins or Blocks you want to reach. You'll face a flock of Fuzzies and a Chainsaw, so if you have Yoshi, it's a good idea to get Wings from the first Block and fly ahead to the yellow Pipe in the sky. If not, ride right and when you reach the Pipe, enter and you'll get Yoshi from the Block inside. The Pipe will lead to another Pipe: enter and you'll find yourself in a new sector of Way Cool. Go right— hitting the Block for Wings if you haven't got them— and fly straight up to Coin heaven! Fly right: no one will attack you, and you're finished when you reach the end. If you have to cross on the Ledges, it's just more of what you faced in the first section.

Awesome: The fourth region of the Special World is an ice zone. Go right, past the ferocious Koopa, taking care to cross the Blocks over the water quickly: it's another accordion Ledge. Skip the Pipe here, but watch out for the Rexes on the bottom of the slopes, and for the Koopas flinging Shells at you from the other side of each. Cross the water ahead; it's followed by a wider water which you can cross *without* activating the P Switch and turning the Coins into Blocks. You're going to want that P Switch in a bit, so just wrap it up and take it with you. Watch out for the sliding Shell that will greet you *immediately* on the other side, along with a parade of Rexes and—when you've passed the next Pipe—a battery of Cheep Cheeps. After the Pipe you'll come to an arch: jump on, use the P Switch here and get the Super Star from above. (You *could* have used the P Switch before, but only if you had a Cape and could get here in a hurry.)

Let's assume you missed getting the Super Star: when you make ready to leap off the second arch, take a *big* jump: a Banzai Bill will zoom in from the right and you'll want to land on top instead of in front of him. Forge ahead: another Banzai Bill will attack within moments. And then another. And another. There are Blurps ahead, but stand on the first Pipe and whack 'em: each one of your Super Star–powered Mario hits will give you a 1-Up! At the end of the level—which is just ahead—you'll be faced with a huge gap. In order to get across, you'll have to let your Starman power run out or you'll kill the very enemy you need! Leap off the back of a Koopa onto the Ledge beyond. Make your jump just to the left of the Dragon Coin and you should have no trouble. After a few dozen tries, anyway.

Groovy: Use the Shell to hit the Block ahead and get Yoshi. There are Koopas strolling ahead: take a head from one and use the rest for duckpins. Next: a Pokey, followed by a Volcano Plant and a Jumping Piranha Plant. If you Y-button it, you can get past all three without stopping. When you cross the Pit, hit the ? when it's a Feather so you'll get a Super Star. If not, you've got your work cut out for you: there are *many* more Pokeys and Plants ahead, and if you aren't invulnerable or haven't got Yoshi to eat 'em up, you've got a problem. There's nothing in the Pipe to the right of the stacked Pokeys, but look out for the Chargin' Chuck throwing Baseballs beyond, a pair of Pokeys, and more Chucks. The end is just beyond them.

Mondo: Things're a little wet here. The Tides come and go, and if you're smart, you'll get up to the left of the first Blurp, then wait until the timer says 251 before leaping on the Blurps and attacking the Amazing Flying Hammer Brother who's chucking Hammers. The Tide will be at its lowest, and you won't have much trouble getting under him, hitting him from his perch, and riding it to the Plateau. The Tide's down again at 219: go past the Jumping Piranha Plant and Blurps. Wait for the Tide to come back so you can reach the ? above. When you reach the next Pipe, stop on top and wait for the next Hammer Brother: appropriate his perch and get off on the next Pipe. When you reach the Block between the set of four Pipes up ahead, wait until the Tide is high so you can jump against it and get the 1-Up. Munchers line the Pits ahead, so you'll want to cross when the Tide is high. The two rows of ? and Blocks ahead will prove very helpful, but the Hammer Brother to the right is not: get in the Water, wait until he's low, and leap up on him. Ride his perch to the Pipe and exit.

Outrageous: The forest is alive with enemies, starting with a Wiggler, Fire Snakes, another Wiggler, and then a Bullet Bill Cannon followed by ten more—the last one's a double-decker. Assuming you don't have a Cape—if you do, just fly over the danger—pick up the Jumping Board and carry it with you. Jump onto the second Cannon and launch yourself to the third, then land on the Bullet Bill itself as it shoots from the fourth, and jump from there to the fourth Cannon. Leap from there right to the *sixth* Cannon, hurry to the seventh, then use the Jumping Board that's there —you're still carrying the first one, right?—to soar to the top of the Blocks ahead and above. Leap from here to the top of the double-decker Cannon. If you need to stop and take stock of things, remember: the Cannons don't fire if you stand right next to them. A Wiggler greets you on the other side of the Pit; use the Jumping Board to vault over it and the mammoth Pipe in front of you. Your leap will carry you over a second Wiggler: alight right under the Hammer Brother, jump up to dislodge him, and ride his perch over the next Pipe. Goombas erupt from the Blocks ahead, so be ready to bop them.

Funky: A Sumo's overhead getting ready to toss lightning down at you, so rush to the right. Piranha in the Pipe ahead, but don't rest when you've cleared it: the rotten vegetable will toss fire at you. So . . . quickly leap onto the Koopa ahead and continue right, but slowly: Sumo alert! Pass when the fire dies down. Two narrow Plateaus with Koopas ahead, then a ?. (After you've had a look at the terrain to here, you can actually get through it with your finger on the Y-button: you'll get to this point *and* the Sumo ahead without stopping once!) Use a head to hit the Block and spring Yoshi. Go ahead, knock off the Sumo Brother, and hit the ?'s: go over the Plateau to the ?'s beyond. The left one will give you a P Switch, which will enable you to liberate Yoshi. After the Pit, you'll come to a row of ?'s and gold Blocks with a row of Note Blocks overhead . . . and a Sumo on them. Jump under him to dislodge him, then spin-jump through the two gold Blocks and butt up under the second Sumo, to the right. Go back to the ? Ledge and hit the last Note Block on the right for a Super Star. Normal Mario hasn't got much of a prayer here. Nothing terribly new—except for the end. You'll reach Coins which spell YOU ARE A SUPER PLAYER!!, and you'll have earned the riches!

A Few Tricks

There are just a few more things about the game you *might* like to know. Tricks, for example.

With Yoshi, go to an area you've won. Go to a Berry and release a power-up you're holding as long as it's *different* from the one you're using. Let Yoshi eat the item *and* the Berry simultaneously. Nothing on the screen will move . . . except your Coin and 1-Up counter. When you're filled to the max, hit start and select.

Another neat trick. If you take a P Switch or a Koopa Shell through an exit, it'll turn into a power-up . . . depending on what kind of Mario you are and what's in your item box. If you need certain items, here's what you can expect:

Normal or Super Mario with no item or with fire or Cape: a Mushroom. With a Mushroom: a 1-Up. Mario with fire but an empty item box, a Mushroom, or a Cape: fire. With fire: a 1-Up. Mario with a Cape but an empty item box or a Mushroom or fire: a Cape. If he's got a Cape, he'll get a 1-Up.

Next: if you ever want to save your game, but the game doesn't give you an option, here's what to do if you have a Cape. Go to the Donut Ghost House, fly to the second floor, and go to the exit. You'll be allowed to save the game there.

Want lots of 1-Ups in the bonus rooms? Instead of jumping up under the Blocks, here's what to do if you have a Cape: Go to the side of each Block in turn and do a spin-jump, hitting the Block with your Cape. You'll cause the Block to register an O . . . three of which in each row will give you a 1-Up!

And, of course, you've probably figured this one out for yourself, but—if you play the two-player game, you can plant one of the Brothers in a favorable place—for example, the midsection of Forest of Illusion 1—and let him collect 1-Ups for the one blazing new trails. When the endangered Brother gets low on lives, his sibling can lap them up and shift them to him. Saves time.

Finally, one very important tip. If you want to get into a Castle or Fortress but can't, all you have to do is press the left and right buttons simultaneously; you'll be able to get into these places even if you don't have the Keys! The one exception is the Valley Fortress. You won't get in Bowser's back door *that* easily!

Rating: B+

Challenge: A

There's a lot to discover, and a lot of new talents to master.

Graphics: B–

The pictures have all the charm of the earlier games, and are very true to the character of those cartridges. However, you expect a *little* more for Super NES. The animation is still a little jerky and the settings are a bit sparse, though levels with three-dimensional backgrounds are very good.

Sound Effects: B–

As with the graphics, the charm is still here, though the effects are not considerably better. The game has a solid if rinky dink musical score,

180

especially the lovely Gilbert and Sullivan-esque theme during the title screen. But was it necessary to make the Super Star music *exactly* the same as a number from *Jesus Christ Superstar*?

Simulation: A

You'll feel like you're doing everything Mario's doing, *especially* swimming.

HOW TO WIN AT SUPER NES GAMES

SUPER R-TYPE

Type: Space shoot-'em-up

Objective: With all the evil planets out in space, you think they'd start bashing each other for supremacy, instead of picking on weak old Earth. Well . . . no such luck. The evil Baido empire—also spelled Bydo in the same instruction booklet—has crushed us under its iron heel. It's up to you and your R-9 fighter to fight through the Baido forces and liberate our world.

Heroes: Your basic ship can fly and shoot; as you travel, you acquire various Lasers, Missiles, and other power-ups.

Enemies: From oncoming ships to Mines to stationary Asteroids with Bases to bosses, the game has all the kinds of foes you've come to expect.

Menu: One player only, though you can select the difficulty level.

Scoring: Points are awarded for ships destroyed and power-ups acquired.

Strategies: Here's the level-by-level lowdown of the low-down invaders:

Space

After the first wave of fighters, you'll get an S from the solo ship you blast. Hit the base on the Asteroid at the bottom, then shift to the one on top. After that, the time-release Mines appear; shoot them down or avoid them, but don't be near the dastardly orbs when they blow! Fortunately, their explosive radius is limited. After a few waves you'll come to twin circles of ships moving around an Asteroid in the center of the screen; there are bases top and bottom. If you can't shoot the circling ships—and you probably won't be able to—take the bottom route and get within them. The reason you want the bottom is that a rather large creature with a sizzling Laser is going to drop from the top of the screen immediately after you pass the Asteroid. You don't want to be up top when that happens. There are a few extra bases to fight on the bottom of the screen, but they're easy. When you near the end of the Asteroid, stay to the far left and save up your B-button power for a good strong burst when the creature's within range. Two should do it; pick up the Laser it leaves behind. There are bases lining the Asteroids top and bottom next; pick either route and clear it out. When you're finished here, boss Illuminator arrives. The boss flits around the screen in a clockwise direction, making it tough to blast. Don't let it trap you on the right, and destroy whatever junk it leaves behind. Use your B-button beam to blast its arms away, then destroy the core.

Ruins

You'll get a Laser and S almost immediately; put the Laser on your nose. You'll have to blast a wave of ships and a base top and bottom before you even enter the Ruins. As you near the entrance of the Ruins, blast the wave of ships that comes out at you with B-button power, then give quick B-button blasts to the giant torpedo-firing ships that appear dead ahead. Pick up the third power-up after you enter, but keep up the B-button fire . . . even if the meter's only shining blue. And be careful: one of these suckers rises up from below and gets behind you! Once you've destroyed the ships, you'll have to pass through three shifting electrical barriers: shoot off their gun emplacements, then ease on through. As in comedy, timing is everything here! You'll get a power-up on the other side and the snake Slimey will rise from the ground: stay to the left and shoot its head, then deal with the bases on top if you have time. Another Slimey rises from the bottom at the same time a wave of ships comes from the top: take out the snake first, then ignore the ships if you like, to concentrate on a third Slimey rising to the right. Two more waves come from bases on the top of the Ruins: fly under them, picking off the ships you can and avoiding their sparse fire. Kill the *Alien*-like things ahead—from the first level—collect the new power-up, and fly straight down the middle. There will be similar waves crawling along the top and bottom and a wave of ships in the middle; your B-button should be sufficiently powered—if you scooped up the M before—to wipe out all of them if you stay in the middle. Get an S ahead, stay low when you clear the narrow section so you can avoid the same foe who dropped in near the end of the first level—with the Laser firing ahead—and get set for the boss, Zabtom. Enter its room quickly: the door closes. (Better it should close behind than *on* you.) The boss fires from an eye on top of the screen and, after a while, opens an eye in its midsection. All the while, killer balls will be rolling off its forehead—if you can call it that—and up from the bottom. Go to the lower eyelid, wait for it to open, blast it, then rise a bit to get out of the way when it fires straight ahead. When it shuts, go down and get ready to repeat. Don't be intimidated when the wall behind you turns into a line of undulating orbs: you stay with your target! (For some bizarre reason, if you watch this level through red and green 3-D glasses, the objects really pop off the Ruins background.)

Cave

Ships come diving at you diagonally from the top and bottom. Fly along the top, just below that outcropping—which will destroy you if you hit it—to get the wave diving from the top right, then go down to get the bottom wave—watching out, though, because the first ship will race right at you, even after it's been hit. Shoot the pod for an S, then stay in the middle, weaving slowly to the right to shoot and/or avoid the converging waves. Normal Y-button fire will take care of these ships. There's another power-up after the Waterfall; go past the falls as soon as they appear so you'll have time to get it. More diving ships follow, from the front and rear—stay on the top of the screen —and then there's a narrow entry ahead, on top: rush through it and get on the bottom for the power-ups. Don't worry: you can blast the cave walls ahead of you down there! Throughout this region Geysers will push you up or down: dart through these when you know the coast ahead is clear. The slugs and vermin won't trouble you much until you reach the "bases" down here: giant mouths that rise from the bottom and descend from the top to spit armies of Crabs at you. Deal with them as you did the normal bases. You'll encounter one on bottom and two on top; after the second one on top, the giant crab Crawlgar lurks ahead. B-button blast it, but it's tough: it'll certainly survive and charge you. Get under it, shoot the base ahead, and attack the giant again when you can—if you have backward-firing weapons, get to its right when the creature shifts left. After you whip it, you'll tangle with Inexsis. Snakes emerge from the sides of the boss, two at a time, and form deadly little circles. Avoid these any way you can, but get back to the boss's left: you've got to shoot a green protuberance that appears now and then. A few hits on that and Inexsis will *exit*.

Giant Space Ship

You'll get S right away, and you'll need it. Drop down fast to avoid the wriggly things that come shooting across the top half of the screen, and blast the walking Ships on the bottom. Stay to the left/bottom to avoid the diagonal Laser from the ship. Move under the Ship as soon as the Missiles start falling from the Ship's underbelly up ahead; pick them off, then line yourself up with the bases attached to the underbelly and shoot the guns off the ships as they fall out. When the second base shuts up, rush past the Ship. (If you've tarried too long under here, portions of the Ship will detach and attack you. These are easily shot . . . unless they drop right on top of you!) Once clear of the ship, *don't* be suckered into rushing up for the power-up above: more wriggly enemies will attack suddenly as you move up there. Wait for the power-up pod to come down. Rise up in the lull between wrigglies and get over the new section of Ship. Homing Missiles and new Ships fly from the top at you; however, with the power-up you get on top, you'll be well equipped to handle them all. Make your way slowly to the right and get up and over this section. Sail diagonally down to the right to avoid the next section of Ship: get under it and keep up a steady fire on its bottom armaments as you move right. Stay to the left of center: you don't want to get fried when the Ship starts to rise and its left-facing thrusters ignite! When you've dismembered the Ship's bottom, you'll be drawn up into its interior to face the boss, Prisoner. It fires a Laser which ricochets off the wall and converges on the left . . . right on you, of course. There are also four guns firing at you from the right. Fortunately, there's a safe zone in here: the lower left corner. Land there and unleash everything you've got at the guns. When they're out, get to the middle of the screen and fire at the boss, shifting left and right to avoid its Lasers or getting back into the lower left corner. It's vulnerable when it retreats to the right.

Mining Field

Get on the bottom and shoot the Gears rolling from the right, then let the ones coming from the top left roll over you: stay halfway up the screen to get the power-up *and* avoid the bullets falling from the overhead Gears. After these encounters you have to weave through a maze that scrolls by itself: get trapped behind one of those orangish buffers and you're finished. Shoot the Gears in the center, dive down for the power-up, then continue to the right, firing at the Gears ahead. Get to the middle and don't worry: your Force power-up will come through the wall behind you and get to you. (Gear bullets cannot, however, penetrate any of the walls here.) Go up and right and blast the Gears coming from the upper right, then drop back to the center after you've cleared the barrier. Back up to the left when the next set of Gears appears on top: let them roll down to you, and blast them as they appear. Go up to the top; you'll get another power-up here. Gears come from behind on the bottom, but your main concern must be the large Ships that come at you from the right. The first one comes from the bottom and rides up, firing; the second, the reverse. Drop down to take out the first one, staying below its cannons and riding up as the Ship does, then take out the second—all the while avoiding the fire from the Gears below. Ahead: Gears drop from the ceiling, but if you stay to the left, they're easily picked off. Another of those big Ships comes from the top right, then from the center, and then, after a walking Ship, from the bottom. This latter one is a bit of a problem in that the Ship's so low, it's difficult for you to stay under it: no maneuvering room down there. Best to be ready with a major B-button blast after the walker appears. Another one appears on the top after that, Gears roll in from behind, and then you've got a tight situation: one big Ship from the top and another from the bottom. Stay dead-center and use your Reflecting Laser Unit—which you should have, or one even more powerful—to fire diagonally at them. The walking Ship on the bottom right is not a threat. Another biggie comes at you from the center, with a power-up hot on its tail. The screen starts to scroll diagonally then: go down and up quickly so you can face the Gears on top and get the power-up. Drop to the bottom to blast the Gears coming from the right, then scoot up to the middle to hit those Gears, then rush to the right along the top—tougher because of the narrow passage up there—or bottom (easier) so you can continue ahead as the screen scrolls. Get to the top if you aren't there already: Gears come from the lower left and top right and a big Ship comes from the middle. You should have Rockets by now; direct your fire at the Gears on top and the big Ship when it appears. Let the Rockets home in on the lower Gears. (If nothing else, being on top will allow the big Ship to sail under you and off the screen to the left: if you're down there, you *have* to destroy it.) *Five* big Ships come next: one top and bot tom, then one center, then one top and bottom. Stay in the center, avoiding the fire of the upper and lower ones, letting your Rockets and Lasers handle them, while you blast the one ahead to give yourself a safe zone. More follow, along with pods dropping from the top and rising from the bottom: just stay on the far left and B-button them all! When you face Rios, there are no patterns to follow: just avoid its fire and shoot it in the center when it's accessible.

Recycling Factory

A flood of Ships attack you here: first from ahead—sweep up and down fast—then from below (B-button them), then in a massive wave from ahead—*definitely* flashing red-level B-button. Once you're inside the Factory, pick off the guns at the bottom and top *and* go to the bottom and hit the Ships there. As you move to the right, blast the Ships or the Elevator platforms ahead. You can't destroy the Elevators, and the supply of Ships seems limitless; so just dart ahead when you can, through the Elevators—watching out for the fire from guns below if your Rockets haven't nailed them—then go to the bottom, shoot the guns there, pick off the ships on the next set of Elevators—watch out: the ones behind you are firing—and rush through those. There are guns top and bottom after that, and blast the ones ahead of you on the bottom and rush up to get the one on top. Ahead: big ships drop *fast* from openings above, coming straight down. Though they *keep* falling out the bottom of the screen, if you're under one, you're dead. Shoot these and stop-and-go past the openings as you can. Stay low here: that gives you more time to back up or dart ahead. The supply of these ships, too, is endless—heckuva military budget the Baido empire has! There are gun emplacements at both the top and bottom, right past these falling whatevers; if you go to the top and bottom before you enter that passageway, your homing Rockets will do a job on them. Another power-up waits just beyond. So do more Elevators, rising up, and blast away as you move ahead. As you go through, walking Ships will come at you along the bottom, so be ready to hit them. Stay low on the screen to avoid the wall on top . . . and to dodge the fire of the gun up top to the wall's right. More big Ships will be falling from above, onto the green Ramp over your head: stay under the Ramp until you've cleared it, collect the power-up to its right, then rise to the upper left—watching out for the falling ships—and go over the Ramp ahead. When you're finished weaving through this region—you'll have to set your own pace: there's no "set way" to get to the other side—you'll face Recycler. The boss has three parts, each of which shoots Lasers and litters the screen with impasses you don't want to hit. Each part has to be destroyed separately by firing at the red "eye" in its center. Again, dart and weave until you have a clear shot and use your heaviest artillery!

Baido Empire

Slimey's back, dropping in from the top left, but before you'll be able to kill it, Crabs will attack you as well. Best to start by saving up for a flashing red B button blast, wait until Slimey's curled up to your right, then take it out with several Crabs. Pick up the power-ups which follow quickly, and get ready for a snake-attack from below. Crabs are *so* plentiful here that you may be tempted to throw the controller at the screen . . . but stick with it! This too shall pass and you'll have a third Slimey to face. Then a fourth coming from ahead. (Until the fourth one come along, one successful strategy is to play to the right center, nearly all the way over, and slide left as Crab attack. When the wave is gone, return to the right and repeat.) After the Slimey from the right, there's another from the top. This is all insanely difficult, and nothing but supersonic reflexes are going to get you through. Assuming you make it through here, and through the narrow tunnel lined with the tortoise-shaped Guardgoyles, the boss Woom isn't appreciably tougher than previous bosses. Shift from left to right on the left side of the screen, avoiding the creature's projectiles while blasting at the twin eggs in the central passageway. Try to blast the giant's arms as well: you'll free companion vessels to help you beat the boss.

If you don't think you can make it all the way through in one sitting, you can execute level select by pressing start at the title screen and, when the game asks you to push start, hold the R button and push the pad up seven to nine times. If you hear a musical measure, your code has been entered. Begin the game, pause it as the action starts: hold R, A, and select simultaneously and push up on the pad to choose your level. (The numbers will change in the lower left.) When you unpause, you'll go to the level you chose. Or maybe you think it's easier to fight your way through? By the way, though the numbers go past seven when you execute the code, all that means is that numbers eleven through seventeen boost the difficulty level.

If you want to give yourself a superpowered ship, do the following on the title screen: press the pad down, hit the R button, press the pad right, down, right, right, down, right, down, down. You'll hear a familiar musical refrain if you did this correctly. Next: start the game, pause it, and push the R button, press the pad right, then down, hit the Y button, press the pad down, right, down, left, right, down, right, right. Now you can choose your power-ups using the R or A, B, X, or Y buttons. (You won't see an options screen: you've got to know what to punch in. A button gives you Sky Attack Laser, B gives you Ground Attack Laser, X gives you Reflect Laser, Y gives you Spread Laser, and R gives you Shot Gun Bomb. A button also gives you Homing Missile and X the Spread Bomb.) If you die during the game—armed like *this* you shouldn't—but if you *do*—just pause the game when you're reborn and program in the second half of the code again. You'll be rearmed when you unpause. Unfortunately, this doesn't work after a continue.

Important note: these work with Nintendo's controllers but not necessarily with any outside controllers you may use.

Rating: B–

Challenge: A

It's a tough game, and unforgiving: mess up and you go back to the beginning of the level.

Graphics: B–

Some impressive animation and detail, but no really startling visuals.

Sound Effects: C

The music is initially powerful, then has an annoying sameness. The explosions, rockets, etc. are just okay.

Simulation: C

The bee-small ship never really convinces that it's a spaceship . . . but the firing is realistic.

ULTRAMAN

Type: Martial arts combat

Objective: For years, Ultraman—incidentally, hero of a long-running Japanese TV series and films—has been battling the evil space virus Gudis. Now the fiend has created mutant monsters on earth, which must be destroyed in hand-to-tentacle combat.

Heroes: Ultraman can use a variety of martial arts moves, leap, and use one of four special weapons. A note about one of them, Burning Plasma: stand close when you use the weapon for it to cause the most damage.

Enemies: These are described in the booklet and are discussed below.

Menu: There is only a one-player game, though you can set the difficulty level.

Scoring: Ultraman plays against a timer—three minutes per battle—and loses energy when hit; points are awarded based on the amount of energy and time left when the monster is destroyed. Points are also

193

awarded for the number of Ultraman lives you have left—you start with three.

Strategies: There's no way to do monster-select in this game. You've got to take them out in sequence, and this is the way to do it:

Stage One: Gudis: The monster fires eyebeams and swings a wicked tail. Keep the pad pressed right and use the X button (Ultra High Jump) and—still holding the pad right but releasing the X button—hit the A button (Ultra High Kick). This combination will weaken and easily destroy the monster: Gudis may never even get off a beam if you keep up a relentless attack. Watch its head (if you can call it that): when it rears back ever so slightly, Gudis is about to fire its eyebeams. Use your Shield when it does so, then move in again. If you can get in close enough, press up on the pad and hit the A button to do an Ultra Spin Kick. The monster may fire its beams several times in succession, so be ready for that.

Stage Two: Bogun: Bogun's got two heads: one on top, with a horn and whiplike antenna, the other on the bottom. The creature spits beams while the top head butts you if you get in close. So: stand back and Ultra High Jump it, with A-button kicks on the way down. When you land on it and inflict damage, hurry back to the left. Bogun is actually easier to kill this way than Gudis was.

Stage Three: Degola: The monster's a big, brown wolf with porcupinelike quills all over its body. It fires rays from its paws, then somersaults over our hero. Naturally, you've got to Ultra High Jump away when it rolls, land on top of its head—giving it a good kick—

and getting away again. If you can stay in close after landing on the monster, Ultra Throw it over your shoulder. A few combinations of these two maneuvers will declaw Degola. When you're in close, a good old-fashioned Ultra Punch will also do serious damage.

Stage Four: Barrangas: This bipedal reptile is a tougher cookie than the previous monsters. It's got rank breath which knocks you down, and small hands that nonetheless pack quite a punch. Ultra High Jump in tandem with a kick in the head is also very effective; since Barrangas moves back when you leap, make sure your jump is long enough. For in-close combat, press up on the pad. When the monster is near, hit Y to use your Shield, then hit Barrangas with an Ultra Upper Cut.

Stage Five: Gudis II: Gudis II has long, deadly arms and spits rings of rays from its head. Like Gudis, its head comes back before it fires. Use the Ultra High Jump and an Ultra Kick when coming down (the X/A combo); when you land, hit the monster with an Ultra Spin Kick. Get away and repeat.

Stage Six: Zebokon: An upright armadillo, the armored monster charges you *fast* and breathes flames. The Ultra High Jump/Kick combination is tough to do here because the monster is so fast. If you can land them, great. If not, Ultra Punch and Ultra Upper Cut are your best weapons . . . in addition to the Ultra Shield to stem its forward progress.

Stage Seven: Majaba: A big, two-legged bug, Majaba leaps and fires rays from its red eyes. The best way to fight this monster is to use an Ultra Upper Cut—saps a lot of its strength—and, when you're too far away, to keep after it with Knuckle Shooter blast after Knuckle Shooter blast. Let your special weapons build up to L4 *only* when Majaba is near defeat.

Stage Eight: Kodalar: This dinosaur with a frog's head and sloth's claws is thick and tough. It uses its swishing tail with a vengeance, and has sizzling eye beams. Ultra Punch is good for in-close fighting but Ultra Throw does a job on Kodalar's strength meter. Because it moves with surprising agility Jumps of all kinds are tough to do . . . though an Ultra Spin Kick will do serious damage if you can land one.

Last Stage: Kilazee: The winged creature leaps and stomps you, and fires rays from its claws and flames from its nose. If you can get in close, Ultra Throw works very well. But since you'll probably want to stay away from Kilazee, use your Special Weapon to cut it down to size; while you let it recharge to L4 for the final blow, use Ultra Chop or Ultra High Jump with a Kick on the way down.

Rating: C
> *Challenge:* C–
>> Though we've suggested numerous ways to beat the monsters, the game gives you a wide variety of moves to learn and use. Unfortunately, the game doesn't give you *nearly* enough for the money: it would have been better if the monsters were bosses and there were other missions to accomplish as well.
>
> *Graphics:* B+
>> Excellent detail, handsome backgrounds, and very good animation.

Sound Effects: B–
   Good punching sounds, explosions, and music.
Simulation: B–
   Some of the moves will make you feel very much like Ultraman, while some will make you feel like a videogamer.

U·N· SQUADRON

Type: Aerial shoot-'em-up

Objective: As a crackerjack top gun pilot, you've got to
strike back at Project 4 terrorists who have attacked
Aslan. To succeed, you've got to fly through ten increasingly dangerous missions.

Heroes: You can choose from one of three pilots, each of
which has special skills: Shin Kazama powers up
quickly; Mickey Scymon is armed to the gills; and
Greg Gates recovers from hits at a rapid pace. Each
pilot can move his plane in any direction, shoot his
Cannon, or use special weapons. These are purchased
from McCoy with cash you earn as you fight through
each mission. (Spelling alert, Capcom: McCoy says,
"You're plane can't handle it." *You're*?!) You also pick
up power-ups as you fly ahead.

Enemies: Lots, from planes to artillery to trucks.

Menu: The game is for one player only.

Scoring: You earn points and money as you play.

HOW TO WIN AT SUPER NES GAMES

Strategies: Here's the lowdown, mission by mission. Note: you can take these in a somewhat different order, but this is the ideal route to build your skills slowly. Though you can also choose your pilot, Shin is recommended.

Front Line Target

For the first and next few missions, go with the Crusader F8E and spend your money on the weapon top left: Cluster. The Helicopters, Artillery, and other enemies here are easy, and there are plenty of power-ups along the way. When you meet the boss, a giant Tank, stay level with the tops of its treads—which will place you below its weapons—and fire away.

Enemy Air Force

Stick with the Crusader and buy the next weapon down, Bomb, along with Megacrush in the lower right—you should have earned enough for both. Stay on the left. Slide up to get the wave coming from the top right, then down for the bottom right attack. After that, slip into the dark blue zone in the center of the screen. The next attack is from behind, but you'll be safe here: pick off the bottom then the top wave as they swoop around and in front of you. Dip down to right above your power meter to tackle the next wave, which comes from behind you, above and below, and fires back at you. Pick up the Mech down there and destroy every enemy on the screen. Get back in the center left for the next wave from behind. Sweep up and down to destroy the wave from the right, then rise on the left to shoot at the giant Jet that drops in the center of the screen. Stay close behind it to get in as many hits as you can. When it reaches the bottom, it will fire back at you; by then, though, it should be on its last legs. A wave from behind, one from the front, then a giant Jet rises from below with a two-plane escort from the left. Blast the small planes then hit the big Jet as before. Another wave from the front —and you've got the general idea. There are more big Jets and waves, followed by the boss: a Stealth Bomber that rises from the bottom left. Stay on the center, left, and drop Bombs on it as it scrolls in. Stay above it. It'll start releasing dum-dum bombs that spray in all directions; you've got to get far from these so you can weave between the pieces, then resume your attack. Stay above or behind it, though, because it will also be dropping bombs.

Aerial Combat Squadron Wolfpack

Stick with the same plane and weapons you've been using. Dart up and down to nail the enemies in front of you, and get above and drop Bombs on the ones who try to sneak in from behind. When they *do* start coming from the left, you'll find yourself playing mostly in the upper left corner, which is fine. Next up: Stealth Fighters coming at you from the front and rear simultaneously. Get out from between them and circle counterclockwise; use Cluster when you're in the midst of them; Bomb them when you're above.

Nuclear Submarine Seavet

Repeat with the plane and arms you've been using. Go down to the lower left and wait. When the Submarine surfaces, use Megacrush. It'll submerge and leap up at you: make sure you get to the upper left while it's submerged! As soon as it's out, nose in the air, get over it and drop Bombs. The Planes that attack won't give you much trouble as you go about your business. However, the Submarine itself will fire Polarislike Missiles when it submerges again, so as soon as it goes under, make your way to the middle of the screen on the top—unless you want to stay on the left and try to shoot them all down as they're fired. Continue right and down, in a clockwise movement, to get around the Missiles when they explode into shrapnel. Stay on the right, center, and back to the left slowly: drop Bombs when the Seavet noses out again. When it flattens out on the surface, get directly over it, to the left of the tower, and use Cluster. Pick off the Missiles it shoots. It'll go down again then and make a Polaris attack just like the first. Go up, right, and down as you did before and repeat until the vessel goes down. If you're having trouble with this level, buy yourself the Thunderbolt and use that instead of Cluster.

Battleship Minks

Switch to the Tomcat for this battle and arm it with Super Shell, Thunder Laser, and Megacrush. The attack comes from the right for several waves, then switches to Dive Bombers from the top center and a Rocket-firing Boat from below. After that you get it from left and right simultaneously. Fly over the Boat in the middle of the screen and stay there for the left/right attack. Another Dive Bomb wave from above, and a Boat firing Missiles from the left; back up to shoot at the former, then stay there and Bomb the latter! After that you get it from everywhere, so just stay on the move. Start firing ahead when the screen goes quiet: that means Minks is heading from the right. Stay one-third of the way up from the bottom of the screen, firing ahead: you've got to hit the Battleship's big guns, and that's the height from which to do it. Thunder Laser will work wonders here, and when the guns are gone, hit the Bridge as you turn and make your second pass at the ship. (If you take out the Bridge first and *kill* the Battleship, you lose out on the money you'd've earned from the guns.) Megacrush is also useful in the first pass over the ship.

Ground Carrier

Take the F20 Tiger Shark and arm it with Phoenix and Falcon Missiles, Bulpup—that's what it says on the screen, folks, though they spell it Bullpup elsewhere—Bomb, and Megacrush. There are Jets above from the right, Tanks below from the right . . . and that's the refrain until you're attacked by Jets from the top left, then top right. After that you get a wave of Helicopters from the right and left, and a giant Helicopter that descends from the center top. Just stay with it, firing from the left. After this there are giant Rocks which you can't fire or fly through—though neither can your enemies. There's a lot of Artillery here, and two more giant Helicopters; the Rocks take some pressure off, though, by blocking a lot of the ground fire while letting you get overhead to drop Bombs. There's a final flurry of Jets from both sides, top and bottom, then a lull before the boss arrives. Stay halfway up the screen so you'll be higher than its deck when it arrives: using Falcon for some downward power, you can shoot down the Missiles and Jets it launches while blasting the launchers themselves; when they're out of commission, train everything on the bridge, which is dead ahead. Megacrush and Bullpup are useful here.

Forest Fortress

The plane of choice here is either Thunderbolt 2, armed to the gills with Napalm, Bomb, Falcon, and Megacrush, or the F20, also fully armed. If you're using the Thunderbolt 2, open up in the middle of the screen on the left, firing ahead and using Falcon to clear away Trees and foes on the ground. When ground bases scroll along, drop to shoot them without letting up on the Falcons. If you're using the F20, you'll have to swing up and down to clear away all the foes. The advantage of the F20 is that you can use the Phoenix—a valuable asset for the assault on the Fortress itself. After you destroy four bases, you'll come to a Missile-launching field. Whichever plane you're using, stay low and pick off the Missiles before they can be launched during this passage; there will be two waves of Jets from the left and one from the right—nothing you can't handle. On the other hand, the Fortress which comes up next *is* a handful! Stay just above the tree line, firing ahead to destroy all of the low-lying guns—which is where Phoenix comes in useful. Get in some shots at the high Turret then scoot over it—unless you're using Phoenix, in which case you can destroy it. Use your special weapons on the next low section, which springs from a shell and sprays Missiles you can easily shoot down. Fly over this and up and over the next dome—getting in as many shots as you can—attack the twin guns up ahead, then swing around and fly left for another go at the Fortress. Finish off all the sections you missed on your first pass. The Missile launcher is the heart of the place, and when it's gone the Fortress is history.

Mountain District Base

Take the Tomcat with Super Shell, Thunder Laser, and Megacrush. Enter the Cave and hit the Jets flying low, then shift to the Guns on the roof of the Cave. Jets will fly in from the left: break off the roof attack to deal with them, then go back to the roof. Shift downward slowly, knocking out the Jets ahead and the Gun on the ground, then swing up and down on the left to shoot the enemies on the right—finishing up on top. There will be an outcropping of Rock ahead, on the ground, with a Gun behind it: when that's under the numeral of your level number (top right), Jets will rocket in from the lower left. Stay in the center and wave through the maze ahead, watching out for enemies front and back. Hang all the way to the left when you see the Lasers firing down from the ceiling and use your own Thunder Laser to destroy them. When you confront the boss, your seasoned eyes will tell you where to hit it: smack in its blue "heart"! Megacrush is extremely helpful here.

The Canyon

Once again, fly the Tomcat, fully armed. At the start, there are Jets top, then Artillery bottom, then Helicopters from behind: a smorgasbord of destruction! Most of the foes thereafter come from the front; play to the left and jump to the Cluster when you're surprised from behind. Blast the large Rock bases ahead, then take to the skies for some serious dogfighting. When the B-1 arrives, stay behind it, Thunder Lasering it; when it comes left, circle it counterclockwise—avoiding its Missiles when you cross it on top—and get behind it again. Now and then it'll blast off the screen to the right, but it will return . . . so be ready!

The Project 4 Fortress

It took all of your skills to get here: now it's going to take all of your skills to get *through* here. The F200 Efreet is suggested. When you slog through to the end, you'll face two bosses: you'll need Falcon Missiles for the first, and Megacrush and Napalm for the second. The first boss drops Guns that will shoot up at you; the upper left will allow you to avoid these while the Falcons destroy them. Meanwhile, just keep up your fire and the boss will go down in flames. The second and final boss is more troublesome. Go to the upper right, weakening your foe with Megacrush, then deliver a flurry of Napalm blasts. When you swing around for a return bout under the boss, fire until you uncover its vulnerable spot: the blue "heart." You won't have any trouble figuring out where it's hidden. Once you've circumnavigated the vessel and turned on it again, unleash Thunder Laser and you should finish it off.

Rating: C+

Challenge: B

The early levels will please newer players, while the later missions will provide a respectable challenge for experienced gamers.

Graphics: C+

So-so animation, and too little detail. The backgrounds range from drab and flat to wonderful.

Sound Effects: C–

Unimaginative score and sound effects.

Simulation: C+

Sometimes you'll feel like you're playing a videogame; sometimes—as when you're fighting the Wolfpack—the illusion of flight is convincing.

WANDERERS FROM YS III

Type: Fantasy quest

Objective: Visiting the town of Redmont, Dogi—whose hometown this is—and Adol find that things are not well. There are monsters in areas outside the town, and strange doings inside. Alone, Adol decides to save the village from its enemies.

Heroes: Adol can walk, leap, duck, and use a sword. As he travels, he acquires various powers which are described in the instruction booklet and below.

Enemies: There are all kinds of foes, and when they die they give you two things: experience points and Gold. Different foes give different rations of each. Note: if you want to get rid of troublesome enemies, simply save the game right before you confront them, and die. When you continue the game, they're usually gone.

Menu: There is only a one-player game.

Scoring: Experience points and Gold are awarded as you play. Your meter is boosted by the number of experience points you get, though the number you have to reach doubles each time until you reach 2000, and then it increases every 2000.

Strategies: The first important things you'll learn are that the Town of Redmont depends on Tigray Quarry—which has become infested with monsters—and that people from the Ballacetine Castle have been lurking about.

Go to the weapons shop and buy a Short Sword, Wood Shield, and Leather Armor, as well as Medicinal Herbs from the apothecary. Talk to the villagers and you'll be sent on a mission: to rescue Edgar from the quarry.

Enter, cut, leap, or duck your way through the hornets and ants here—using upthrust to slay hordes of the former—and you can either fight your way down the stairs or drop down, falling several flights to avoid fights (though you won't collect Gold). On the bottom level go right and watch out for more of the ants. Cross another bridge to more blue warriors, climb the stairs and go right, leap the blue jelly—you can't kill it unless your experience points are in the 800 range—leap the next two, then go to the Treasure Chest up ahead. You'll be rewarded with Robert's Pendant. Head down the stairs and go right. You'll bump into a Duey, a youngster who will give you the Warehouse Key: you can use it to get a powerful Long Sword. Return to the stairs, go up and left, past the jellies, and go down the stairs. When you come to the blue warriors, kill them to build up experience: push down on the pad to crouch and just keep hitting the Y button. They won't touch you; inch forward between attacks. Go back to the first area where you met blue warriors, go *left* on the bottom, and collect a Power Ring from the Treasure Chest. Don't use it yet, however. Climb the stairs, and when you get to the topmost right level, leap up to the cliff . . . then leap up again. The Warehouse is hidden on the right. Inside, you face Dulan; win here and the Long Sword is yours. If you've got 2000 experience points and one Herb, you'll win. Just kneel and stab away.

If you have trouble here, enter and leave the Quarry several times to build your experience points; each time you exit, your strength will return to full. It's also a good idea to go back to town and buy Chain Main for 1500 Gold when you've earned enough, as well as Medicinal Herbs. (If you want to just kill the fiends near the front, you can constantly go back out and recharge. For example, go to the lower level of the first walkway right inside the Quarry. Kill the two ants there and stand facing right and the lower right bottom. Do the Y button and up on the pad for rapid upthrust and just mow down every hornet that flies in from the right. There'll be a lot of them! You can also nail blue warriors by crouching on the third ledge down on the left, on the right side facing left, and mowing down the fighters coming from the left. (Just make sure the left side of the ledge is off the screen; if it isn't, leap to the right ledge, then come back.)

When you've won at the Warehouse, return to Duey and go down the stairs, drop down the pit, and go right at the bottom. Ton of jellies to kill as you drop down more shafts and continue right. There's a new boss ahead; however, you don't want to go here yet. Go back to town and get more Herbs, as well any Armor you can afford.

When you fight the boss at the bottom of the Quarry, press up, then press B-button, then A-button (jump and slash) right under the fiend. Make sure you have one Herb and are at least at 6000 points. You'll be rewarded with a Sun Statue for your Inventory list, and the door will open ahead of you. Enter and rescue

Edgar. You, he, and Duey will be spirited to the front of the Quarry.

Back in town, take the Robert's Pendant to his mother: she'll give you the Shield Ring in return. Also, buy stronger weapons. Go to the tavern and listen to Ellena tell the story of Chester and Cleric Pierre: you'll be learning what you need to know to go to Ilvern. Inside, the flying, flaming heads are easy to dispatch: kneel to the left of the third Candelabra, facing left, and mow down the Sorcerers as they enter. Build yourself up to 8000 experience points and get Gold to buy goods in town.

Back in the ruins at Ilvern, go right, down the steps, and right, crouching whenever you have to fight the fireball-throwing Wizards. When you exit, birds swoop down from trees, so be ready to make like another bird (duck!) and slash at them. If you want, stand just to the right of the second tree and use Y and press up on the pad: you'll mow them down. It'll cost you hit points, but you'll get to 10,000 experience points in no time, and can recharge simply by going to the front gate of the ruins.

After the birds, you'll face fiends with whips. Drop down the two cliffs you come to, fight the giant Crabs —kneel the whole time and you'll be okay—and enter the next set of ruins, to face the flaming faces again. You want to get through here quickly and hopping: in addition to the faces and Wizards, there are fireballs scooting along the floor. The Chest downstairs will give you a Small Shield—no help if you already bought the Large Shield! When you exit, you'll be in a hallway: eavesdrop on what Pierre has to say.

You'll be dropped into a sea of Lava for your efforts: race to the left, jumping the rolling insects and staying ahead of the Firebirds behind you. Drop down and go left on the cliff: Herb Medicine is growing there. Drop down and go right. A huge flame snake will leap up from the ground at you: run/leap to stay ahead of that as well! Another snake—this one looking more like a dragon—will attack in the next section. With your hand on the Herb button, stab up repeatedly from any vantage point, attacking its head, and refill when you get low. If you bought the Amulet —you should have—use it here. When you defeat the Firedragon Gilan, you'll be rewarded with the Fire-dragon's Amulet . . . but don't tackle the fiend un-less your experience points are 12,000 or more. Retrace your steps after that and go back through the first fire snake's area—if you time it right, you can run under the flaming monster and, when the terrain changes, leap over it, without ever being hit—and go back up the slope (you can jump back up by standing on the highest point below it). When you come to the sea of Lava, hold out Pendragon's Amulet and the molton rock will solidify. Cross to the right, through areas with more Firebirds and coiled, rolling insects, and you'll come to a flight of stairs. Climb and talk to your old ladyfriend in the room up ahead. She'll take you to a safe place: eavesdrop as Chester and Lord Garland discuss their plans for Cleric Pierre. When you and Ellena are free to speak again, you'll find a Statue nearby. Move it and enter the chamber beyond.

The first corridor is safe, and so is the second Lava region. When you enter the second region, though, you'll face a huge winged reptile that spits fire. To fight it, use the Amulet—go back and get another if you don't have one—the Shield Ring, and have a Me-dicinal Herb at the ready. Stand on the highest cliff to the left. Lure the monster over by running down to the right, then run back to the cliff. You'll be rewarded with the Star Statue when you win here.

Go back to the left and talk to Chester and Ellena. She'll take you back to town, where you should buy another Amulet, Herb, recharge your Ring, and talk to Dogi. He'll tell you he's going to the Eldam Mountains to meet with his master. He'll also tell you to have a word with Edgar. At Edgar's house you'll learn about thieves from Ballacetine Castle. You'll also receive the Time Ring.

Go back to the Quarry, climb down the Pit with all the blue warriors, and go *left*. Enter the door to the Cursed Mine and join the others down there. There are plants with deadly tentacles here—wait till those are extended, then slash them—warriors with *very* long swords (you'll take some damage, even if you crouch). Continue left and you'll find a Chest with the Shining Crystal. When you've got that, go back to town. Use that Crystal to whip up some Brocia's Secret Medicine at the apothecary, buy a Broad Sword for 8000 Gold, then return to the Cursed Mine. Continue until you come to the walkway with a hole in it. Drop down and crawl under the walk. There's a pit: go down, using the Mirror of Illusion to freeze the second plant if you can't kill it, then keep going down. When you get the Mission's Tablet from the Chest, go left. Follow the path down; make sure you stop at the Chest with the Plate Mail in it—if you fell down the blue warrior pit, you missed it: it's in the cavern to the left of that, on top. When you've donned it, go to the blue warrior pit: a ledge on the left side will lead you to another corridor. To get to that passageway, simply climb the cliff on the left, above the ledge. Go left, drop down the stairs, and go right to fight the monster Galbalan. You've got to leap up to the ledge where the monster is and just whack away at it. You'll need to be at 30,000 experience points to succeed—or at least have a full meter in the 20,000 range and an Herbal refill!

When you slay the beast, you'll be rewarded with the Flash Statue. Return to your friend, waiting outside the Cursed Mine, and he'll tell you to go back and see Edgar.

Before you talk to Edgar, you'll overhear what the corrupt Lord McGaya has to say to him. Then Edgar will give you a letter to take to the hermit in the Eldam Mountains. So, after restocking your depleted supplies, off you go!

Climb the peaks, but watch out for monsters that erupt from clear patches of snow . . . and, in the second screen, from the rock itself! Inside the Mine, the monsters are bigger and tougher than you're used to, so move with caution. Some burst from the ground, others fly by, others stroll along. All deal in very quick death. To deal with the giant Hornets when you're in a pit, go left and they'll follow—then dash ahead to the right. As for the giant worm-things, if you crouch, they'll ignore you *and* you can duck their ejecta. When you reach the snowy region, go to the cabin—no monsters here—and have a chat with Dogi and the hermit.

The hermit will tell you about an important Statue, about a Key to get it, and about the monster that owns the Key. He'll give you a Banded Sword, and you'll continue toward the right. When you fight your flying foe, use Power Ring, Amulet, and take a flying leap at her before she takes off. Since your Power Ring will be running down, you don't want to waste too much time chasing her down. Run back and forth between the steep slope on the far right and the small peak to its left. Try to keep her in there, since you can leap at her from the slope. You want to be at 40,000 experience points when you take her on. It's also a good idea to have the Banded Armor here (12,000 Gold). When you beat her, you'll get the Judgment Staff . . . even though it's spelled "judgement" on the screen. (Note: if you have to go back through the Mine to get to town, make sure you stop in the Hermit's house on your return. Your strength meter will be fully restored, free of charge!) Stop at the Stone Statue on the way out and watch as the ground melts away beneath it: drop down and go right.

Wonderful: another Mine with more of the same monsters you fought before. On the other side of the first Mine is a nice big Dragon, spitting fire. Stand directly under its head—approximately the length of your hero from the depression in the ground to the left—and leap up constantly: Y-button, B-button jockeying while you press the pad up. As long as you keep smacking its jaws, it won't spit fireballs or swish its tail—the latter being instantly lethal. And don't count on the Amulet helping you here: it does absolutely nothing! You'll get the Dark Statue when you beat the fire-breather.

As you turn to go, an old friend will come by for a chat . . . and you'll be trapped with him thanks to a cave-in. But Chester will join your team and you'll be spirited back to the town, where you'll learn that everyone's been abducted by the rotten folks from Ballacetine Castle. Naturally, you're about to head there, with the Healing Ring in your possession. Go talk to Edgar; that will open the path to Ballacetine Castle.

The first hall is foe-free; downstairs, though, you'll face chitinous things that sap a whole lot of strength when they hit you. Climb the stairs at the end and face a tentacled ugly. Up more stairs there are armored guards, also *très* powerful: on top of that, you have to slide under or leap over the weapons of a pair of Statues in the hall. Up the stairs at the end, and—you see those Spears rising from the floor? You'll face more of them above, only this time you'll *have* to leap them. Down the stairs at the end, cross more Statues and guards, another set of Spears, and climb the stairs at the end. Watch when you climb, though: the Spears rise up through the steps! At the end of the next corridor, there are Spears and steps: beyond the Spears is a door. Don't enter yet, but remember where it is. Climb and enter the door on top. Cross the room—no foes here—and enter the next one. Leap the Spears, climb the stairs, go right on top, climb the next stairs, go left, and dispatch the guard so you can open the Chest. (Kill the guard after leaping it; otherwise, there will be an endless parade of them.) You'll get the superpowerful Battle Shield from the Chest.

Upstairs: kill the guard by stabbing up before you're fully out of the stairwell. Slip past the Statue, then another, then get set to stop-and-go through Statues and Spears. Go up the stairs and face the music! Or rather . . . the bolo-swinging boss. Crawl right to the monster's side and smack it repeatedly, using your Power Ring, to defeat it. When the giant dies, it will give you the Garnet Bracelet. Turn the Bracelet onto the Blue Knight Jilduros behind that door you saw before but didn't enter: he'll be freed and will leave the Great Chamber. Continue to the right, go down, and get the Battle Armor from the Chest downstairs. Go back up and right, into the Courtyard, to face a fire-breathing hound. Just hack away and leap it and, when you win, continue right to the Music Hall.

Much to your horror, you'll learn that Ellena is a prisoner. But you can do nothing until you finish cleansing the castle. Go through the door that opens here, go down, and fight three of the tentacled monsters you faced before—stand out of range as they fire their blue bullets, then race to their centers to stab them. Stop in front of the Dungeon to talk to the prisoner, then go right, climb the stairs, and face Jilduros, who has the Key to the Dungeon. (Some thanks you get for having liberated him!) Wait until he comes from his dome—otherwise, he will kill you—and hit at him when his axe is drawn back: two hits, then withdraw, two hits, withdraw, etc. He'll surrender the Key when he dies: go and open the door to the Dungeon. Inside you'll find Robert and Cleric Pierre. Talk to them, then go to the right side of the Dungeon and talk to the soldier there. He'll give you the Blue Bracelet.

Go back to where you fought Jilduros, climb the stairs and go right. Enter the door at the end and enter the Clock Tower. There are more *very* big guards here, and blobs crawling around on the clockworks overhead. Climb the stairs, but kill the guard overhead from below . . . before you emerge onto his narrow platform. (If you stand on the third step from the top, you'll be okay.) There's a guard shooting at you from the left: leap to the Gear when the gun is firing away from you and kill the soldier before he can fire down. Make your way left and right until you've climbed all the Gears: there are two more gunmen and more blobs to deal with, but they won't present much of a problem. Exit on the top right. More Gears in the next room; cross directly to the right and up slightly and open the Chest to obtain the Flame Sword. Go left, get on the Chain, and ride it down. Cross the Gears *above* the blob on the right, drop down on the right, and exit through the door there. Three guards attack in a row, and when you get above them and head left on the Gears, there's a shooter to worry about. Crawl right—killing the two blobs—go up, kill more blobs, defeat the marksman on top, and exit. Next room: you'll be told by one of the big golden guards to turn back or perish. Being a bold sort, you don't take the warning seriously. When you beat him—the Mirror of Illusion will stop the guy cold and let you chop him to pieces—a Chain will descend from the ceiling, carrying you to the Bell House. At least there are no foes here. Go right. Ellena will meet you and give you the great news that

Galbalan has revived. But is it really Ellena? Not on your life. It's a monster. If you've used your Amulet, get behind the giant and hit it with three quick slashes. It will dematerialize; run to the left—middle of the screen—and wait for it to reappear facing right: hit it again from behind, run all the way to the left, and so on. Be ready to leap its lightning bolts which become lighting *balls* and roll after you. Note: if you don't like where the giant has materialized (i.e., facing you), run in the opposite direction while he's still forming; usually, the monster will relocate.

You'll be rewarded with the Evil Night Spell when you beat the titan. Your quest is nearly at an end, Adol, and the lady yours! But first, it's on to—

Gabalan's Island. You'll go back to redmont first, huddle with Edgar and get the Ogre's Ball of Fire, then use it to throw some light on the dark island. Inside the maze, get to the moving ledge, go down, and stay put when it stops the first time. When it stops the second time, get off on the left and push the pad left. let yourself go down/left until you meet the second incarnation of Garland. Fight as before, using the Fairy Necklace for added power.

This isn't called Gabalan's Island for nothing, however. Soon you'll be facing the big G, and here's how to win: use your sword to destroy Gabalan's hands *first*, then wait until the orb appears in its mouth. Use the Amulet three times, then jump up and hit the orb with your sword to slay the creature. Not too difficult, is it?

Rating: B
> *Challenge*: A
>> The Zelda-like game will keep you hopping for a while!
> *Graphics*: B
>> Though cartoony, the graphics are well done.

Some of the three-dimensional landscapes are extraordinary.

Sound Effects: C

Excellent theme song, but otherwise just okay music, fair sound effects.

Simulation: C

Nothing special; you won't feel any different with a ton of armor and weapons as when you had none!

THE ULTIMATE GUIDES TO
THE ULTIMATE HOME ENTERTAINMENT SYSTEM

HOW TO WIN AT
NINTENDO® GAMES

Jeff Rovin

Let legendary videogame expert Jeff Rovin show you the way to complete mastery of the Nintendo videogame system! Each guide contains tactics, techniques, and winning strategies for some of the most popular Nintendo games! And each guide has *all-new* games in it!

HOW TO WIN AT NINTENDO GAMES
_____ 92018-0 $3.95 U.S. _____ 92019-9 $4.95 Can.

HOW TO WIN AT NINTENDO GAMES II
_____ 92016-4 $3.95 U.S. _____ 92017-2 $4.95 Can.

HOW TO WIN AT NINTENDO GAMES III
_____ 92215-9 $3.95 U.S./$4.95 Can.

HOW TO WIN AT NINTENDO GAMES IV
_____ 92721-5 $3.99 U.S./$4.99 Can.

Unofficial guides—not endorsed by Nintendo®. Nintendo is a registered trademark of Nintendo of America Inc.

Publishers Book and Audio Mailing Service
P.O. Box 120159, Staten Island, NY 10312-0004
Please send me the book(s) I have checked above. I am enclosing $ _____ (please add $1.50 for the first book, and .50 for each additional book to cover postage and handling. Send check or money order only—no CODs) or charge my VISA, MASTERCARD or AMERICAN EXPRESS card.

Card number _____

Expiration date _____ Signature _____

Name _____

Address _____

City _____ State/Zip_____
Please allow six weeks for delivery. Prices subject to change without notice. Payment in U.S. funds only. New York residents add applicable sales tax.

NINS 9/91